Task Force Report No. 82

Securing Space
A Plan for U.S. Action

Nina M. Armagno and Jane Harman, *Chairs*
Esther D. Brimmer, *Project Director*

The mission of the Council on Foreign Relations is to inform U.S. engagement with the world. Founded in 1921, CFR is a nonpartisan, independent national membership organization, think tank, educator, and publisher, including of *Foreign Affairs*. It generates policy-relevant ideas and analysis, convenes experts and policymakers, and promotes informed public discussion—all to have impact on the most consequential issues facing the United States and the world.

The Council on Foreign Relations takes no institutional positions on policy issues and has no affiliation with the U.S. government. All views expressed in its publications and on its website are the sole responsibility of the author or authors.

The Council on Foreign Relations sponsors Task Forces to assess issues of current and critical importance to U.S. foreign policy and provide policymakers with concrete judgments and recommendations. Diverse in backgrounds and perspectives, Task Force members aim to reach a meaningful consensus on policy through private deliberations. Once launched, Task Forces are solely responsible for the content of their reports. Task Force members are asked to join a consensus signifying that they endorse "the general policy thrust and judgments reached by the group, though not necessarily every finding and recommendation." Members' affiliations are listed for identification purposes only and do not imply institutional endorsement. Task Force observers participate in discussions, but are not asked to join the consensus.

For further information about CFR or this Task Force, please write to the Council on Foreign Relations, 58 East 68th Street, New York, NY 10065, or call the Communications office at 212.434.9888. Visit our website, CFR.org.

This report is printed on paper that is FSC® Chain-of-Custody Certified by a printer who is certified by BM TRADA North America Inc.

FSC
www.fsc.org
MIX
Paper | Supporting
responsible forestry
FSC® C101537

TASK FORCE MEMBERS

Task Force members are asked to join a consensus signifying that they endorse "the general policy thrust and judgments reached by the group, though not necessarily every finding and recommendation." They participate in the Task Force in their individual, not institutional, capacities.

Nina M. Armagno
Lieutenant General, USSF, Ret.

Charles F. Bolden Jr.
The Charles F. Bolden Group

Esther D. Brimmer
Council on Foreign Relations

Laetitia de Cayeux
Global Space Ventures

Phaedra Chrousos
Libra Group

Mai'a K. Davis Cross
Northeastern University

Laura DeNardis
Georgetown University

Charles Duelfer
Independent Consultant

Celeste V. Ford
Stellar Solutions, Inc.

Stephen J. Hadley
Former National Security Advisor

Jane Harman
Former U.S. Congresswoman

Kay Bailey Hutchison★
Former U.S. Ambassador to NATO

Rob Meyerson
Interlune

Robert B. Millard
Massachusetts Institute of Technology

Chris Morales
Point72 Ventures

Jamie Morin
The Aerospace Corporation

Saadia M. Pekkanen
University of Washington

Audrey M. Schaffer
Slingshot Aerospace

Benjamin L. Schmitt
University of Pennsylvania

Jonathan Spalter
USTelecom

Kathryn D. Sullivan
Potomac Institute for Policy Studies

Ezinne Uzo-Okoro
Harvard University

Samuel S. Visner
Space Information Sharing and Analysis Center

★The individual has endorsed the report and contributed a concurring opinion.

CONTENTS

vi   *Foreword*
viii *Acknowledgments*

2   EXECUTIVE SUMMARY

6   INTRODUCTION

14 FINDINGS

28 RECOMMENDATIONS

44 CONCLUSION

46 *Concurring Opinion*
47 *Endnotes*
53 *Acronyms*
55 *Task Force Members*
67 *Task Force Observers*
72 *Contributing CFR Staff*

FOREWORD

When the Soviet Union launched the Sputnik I satellite into space in 1957, the world changed. Not only was a domain once thought to be unexplorable suddenly within reach, but that "Sputnik moment"—a realization the United States was at risk of losing its edge to an adversary in a strategic environment—catalyzed a commitment from the president to embrace space as a national priority. In a speech at Rice University, President John F. Kennedy declared that the United States would "choose to go to the moon in this decade." As a result of the prioritization of this objective, we did, and we took the steps necessary as a country to ensure the United States would be the world's leading space power.

During the height of the space race and the years that followed, activities in space were largely limited to a handful of governments, at times acting in tandem with one another. That is no longer the case. Indeed, the number of actors in space has grown to more than ninety countries with nonstate actors, namely private companies, accelerating innovation and opening the door for more governments to launch their assets into space, including constellations of satellites. To address the changing nature of space, the Council on Foreign Relations convened a Task Force on Space Management Policy.

The international organizations and treaties currently governing space were not designed with the proliferation of actors and the rapid rise in space traffic in mind. As the international system exists currently, there is no single multilateral body capable of managing space traffic on its own.

The Task Force finds the boom in satellites and debris in low Earth orbit (LEO) especially concerning, as space becomes more and more crowded. Just since 2018, satellites in LEO have doubled, while space debris greater than 10 cm in diameter has topped more than 40,000 items.

Left unaddressed, this reality risks collisions between the space assets of China, Russia, the United States, and others becoming all the more likely. At the same time, China and Russia show interest in expanding their anti-satellite capabilities, which if used would threaten U.S. security and economic interests—and dramatically increase the potential amount of debris, further accelerating the risks and, without mitigation, potentially rendering space unusable by all.

If the United States fails to adequately reshape its approach to space, it risks abdicating its position as the world's leading space power. A new presidential administration and a new Congress, however, present an opportunity for the United States to reaffirm its commitment to leading in space, and the rapidly changing nature of space—which will only accelerate further—makes the challenge all the more pressing.

Thus, the Task Force proposes a response based on seven principles: making space a top national priority; revitalizing American international leadership; fixing the vulnerability of space assets and enhancing deterrence; sharpening policy on China while also seeking strategic engagement on hotline issues; building on existing international regimes to improve space traffic management; incorporating the commercial sector and other relevant nonstate actors; and treating space as a global commons.

This report offers a pragmatic prescription on how the United States should best confront the changing nature of space, and I commend the Task Force members for their commitment to forging a way forward for enhanced U.S. leadership and better international coordination in space. I thank the co-chairs, retired Lieutenant General Nina Armagno of the U.S. Space Force and former Congresswoman Jane Harman, for their leadership. I also thank CFR's Esther Brimmer, who directed the Task Force and authored the report, and Anya Schmemann, who shepherded the process.

Michael Froman
President
Council on Foreign Relations
February 2025

ACKNOWLEDGMENTS

This report is the result of the dedication of the members and observers of the Task Force on Space Management Policy, who devoted their time and expertise to examining the interdisciplinary and multifaceted issues surrounding space governance and offering pragmatic solutions. I am grateful for the opportunity to have worked with such an impressive and dynamic group of experts.

I would especially like to thank our distinguished co-chairs, Lieutenant General Nina Armagno and the Honorable Jane Harman. Their leadership, guidance, and thoughtful insights helped the Task Force engage in innovative discussions and create a thorough and compelling report. It was an honor and a privilege to work with them.

Throughout this process, I was inspired by the robust dialogue and thoughtful comments shared during our Task Force meetings and related discussions. I am deeply grateful for the contributions of each Task Force member and observer. Their depth of expertise and the range of vantage points enriched our deliberations and the report. Task Force member Stephen Hadley deserves special recognition for sparking the initial idea for this Task Force and helping to refine and share the report.

Our report benefited from consultations with senior officials at NASA, the National Security Council, and the National Space Council, as well as in the U.S. Department of Commerce, the Department of Defense, and the Department of State. I extend a special thank you to the Department of State's Bureau of International Organization Affairs.

This report was informed by a research trip to international organizations in Vienna and Brussels in June 2024. I am grateful to our co-chairs for expertly leading this trip, as well as the senior officials from the EU Space Surveillance and Tracking, the North Atlantic Treaty Organization, the United Nations Office of Outer Space Affairs, the United Nations Committee on the Peaceful Uses of Outer Space, and experts from the European Space Policy Institute and the Centre for European Policy Studies, all of whom met with our delegation and shared their unique perspectives on these evolving issues. We also met virtually with officials from the International Telecommunications Union. Although we have sought the advice of many in the making of this report, I am ultimately responsible for its content.

I would like to recognize the indispensable contributions of my colleagues at CFR, without whom this report would not be possible. I would like especially to thank Anya Schmemann, managing director of the Task Force Program, whose wisdom and expertise guided this process, and her teammates Chelie Setzer and Katerina Viyella, who supported the coordination and preparation of this report every step of the way. I also extend my thanks to Senior Fellow Stuart Reid for his thoughtful editorial comments and Senior Vice President and Director of Studies Shannon O'Neil for her careful reviews.

Thanks are due to the Product, Design, and Publications teams, who expertly organized and prepared this report for its final publication. Particularly, I would like to thank the team that helped make the graphics and data visualizations that help the report come to life. I am grateful for the research conducted in support of this report by Research Associate Julia Katsovich, as well as by several hardworking interns.

Finally, I thank CFR President Michael Froman for his recognition of space governance as a vitally important and relevant issue for the Task Force to address and for affording me the opportunity to direct this endeavor.

Esther D. Brimmer
Project Director

TASK FORCE REPORT

EXECUTIVE SUMMARY

It is impossible to overstate the importance of space to the United States. For Americans, modern life depends on information from the thousands of satellites orbiting the globe, allowing people to do everything from navigating their cars by GPS to growing crops and managing inventory. Satellites are also essential to U.S. national security, enabling the United States to communicate with its military forces, gather intelligence, warn of a potential nuclear attack, and more.

Space is a strategic vulnerability. The United States has more strategic assets in space than any other country. Almost as important, dynamic American companies—particularly SpaceX—have revolutionized space, placing in orbit thousands of commercial satellites on which the U.S. economy increasingly depends. But other countries are following suit. China in particular is on track to have thousands of its own satellites in orbit in the not-too-distant future.

Further complicating matters, the space assets that the United States already has—mostly satellites, but also ground stations and modes of communication—are increasingly vulnerable now that China and Russia have developed the means to divert, disable, or destroy them. The methods include electronic warfare and jamming as well as direct-ascent anti-satellite (ASAT) missiles.[1]

Space is a strategic challenge. Space is becoming more congested by the year. Since 2018, the number of satellite payloads orbiting in low Earth orbit (LEO)—that is, objects below an altitude of 1,200 miles—has more than quadrupled.[2] Then there is space debris—defunct objects or fragments of human-made materials. Over 40,000 items of space debris greater than 10 cm in diameter now orbit Earth at speeds of up to 18,000 miles per hour. This increase in space traffic and space debris makes collisions more likely. It also threatens the lives of astronauts on the International Space Station (ISS) and on the space stations being constructed by China and Russia. China, Russia, and the United States are the source of most of that debris and share an interest in avoiding collisions, but they are also wary of one another's intentions.

Unlike aviation, shipping, and telecommunications, the space economy has no single international institution that can issue legally binding rules to address congestion risks. If the current moment were a period of tranquility among the great powers, it would be easier to develop rules to enhance the safety, security, and efficiency of human activity in space. The confluence of innovation in the commercial space economy, an increase in the number of countries with civil space programs, and ongoing geostrategic tensions make the task of developing globally accepted rules more complex, but also more necessary than ever.

Therefore, space is a strategic imperative. In the increasingly chaotic realm of space, the United States' position is slipping. In 1957, the Soviet Union's launch of the Sputnik satellite was a wakeup call, spurring the United States to assume a dominant role in space. Today, nearly seventy years later, the United States is in danger of losing that privileged position. In many ways, the country risks another Sputnik moment.

The United States needs to act now to address threats to space assets; champion space traffic management to support the growing space economy; and incorporate commercial perspectives into civilian and national security space policy.

Findings

1. U.S. leadership in space is critical to U.S. national security, to U.S. global leadership, to U.S. hard and soft power, and to the security and prosperity of the American people.

2. Space traffic management is crucial to the well-being of modern human societies. Actions taken—or not taken—now will shape human activity in space for decades. Without changes in how humans use space, the benefits of access to space could be lost to everyone.

3. U.S. space assets are increasingly vulnerable to attacks by China, Russia, and other potential adversaries—attacks that could come from the ground, the air, or space itself.

4. While the United States remains the leading space power across the civil, commercial, and national security realms, China is emerging as a peer competitor.

5. Current international organizations and treaties are ill suited to the new realities of space activity, and no single multilateral body is designed to comprehensively manage space traffic.

6. The expertise and perspective of the private sector and other nonstate actors is critical to effective space traffic management.

7. In an era of increased competition in space, the United States may not always be the first to reach new destinations in space. Therefore, the United States benefits from the principle in the Outer Space Treaty that outer space "is not subject to national appropriation by claim of sovereignty."

Recommendations

1. **Make space a top national priority.** U.S. President Donald Trump should demonstrate this commitment by convening a space summit in the first year of his administration and reassessing priorities to include whether to declare key space systems to be "critical infrastructure."

2. **Revitalize American international leadership in space.** The president should instruct relevant cabinet officers that the United States is to lead the world in space and make this a personal priority as well. The president should structure the National Security Council staff to support the president in this role and the national effort to lead in space. The National Space Council, formed under the first Trump administration, could be utilized.

3. **Fix the vulnerability problem and enhance deterrence.** To do so, the president should consider a number of steps, including enhancing domain awareness, proliferating and widely distributing space assets to increase their resiliency, hardening space assets against various modes of attack, providing space assets with defensive capabilities, and developing replacement assets that can be deployed quickly when needed. To develop such options, the president should launch a space vulnerability, remediation, and deterrence assessment that includes participation by the Department of Defense, the intelligence community, private sector space companies, and representatives of civil space organizations and academic institutions, among other groups.

4. **Sharpen policy on China and seek strategic engagement on hotline issues.** Along with its measures to compete successfully with China in space, protect U.S. space assets from disablement or destruction by China, and deter China from undertaking such actions, the U.S. government should conduct a targeted space-related engagement with China on "hotline" communications, space traffic management, and the rescue of spacefarers in distress. The Trump administration should work with Congress to enact any necessary additional legislation or changes in existing legislation required to facilitate this effort.

5. **Build on existing international regimes to improve space traffic management.** This effort should involve developing "rules of the road" to deconflict space activities, avoid collisions and other accidents, and mitigate risk from space debris. And it should involve U.S. allies, partners, and even adversaries. This system would draw upon existing international entities, including the UN Office for Outer Space Affairs (UNOOSA) and the International Telecommunication Union (ITU).

6. **Incorporate the commercial sector and other relevant nonstate actors.** The United States should lead efforts with its partners to establish a regularly scheduled forum or advisory group that channels expertise from the commercial sector, civil society, and academia into the deliberations of international organizations responsible for managing space traffic and into related diplomatic efforts. In addition, along with the United States, spacefaring states should create an international "companion" group that connects private sector and nongovernmental organizations to UNOOSA and the ITU.

7. **Treat space as global commons.** Space should not be subject to national territorial claims but rather remain open to all nations. The United States should make clear that it treats space as the common inheritance of all humanity and encourage other states to do so as well. To that end, the United States should urge all countries to sign and ratify the 1967 Outer Space Treaty.

INTRODUCTION

Space is a critical strategic domain—just like oceans and airspace. Space assets are vital to modern life, underpinning the United States' security and prosperity. In the past five years, however, conditions in space have changed drastically, raising new problems that demand new solutions. In an earlier era, space activities were dominated by a few countries implementing government-led programs. But those days are gone.

For one thing, the number of actors has proliferated. Private companies have become the drivers of innovation and activity in space, injecting ingenuity and efficiency into the U.S. government's space program. Newer companies can execute fixed-price contracts—which do not cover cost increases—faster and for less money than legacy manufacturers, which are accustomed to a cost-plus fee payment model that allows the company to pass cost overruns on to the government agency purchaser.[3] The availability of private sector launches has, in turn, opened space to more governments. Over ninety countries now have assets in space providing services or observing Earth (see figure 1).[4] The list of countries includes China and Russia, both U.S. adversaries. China has launched its own crewed Earth-orbiting space station and landed two uncrewed spacecraft on the far side of the Moon. Russia plans to cooperate with China on the International Lunar Research Station. But friendly countries also see space programs as a mark of great-power status. India, for example, has landed a device near the lunar south pole and has made clear it wants to be included in making decisions regarding use of the Moon.

As more governments and companies send more objects into space, that realm has become increasingly congested. Since 2018, the number of satellites orbiting in LEO has doubled, fueled by the dramatic expansion in private sector transport and service providers.[5] The number of

Figure 1

U.S. and Other Countries Are Launching More Objects Into Space
Satellites and other objects launched into space, by commissioning country

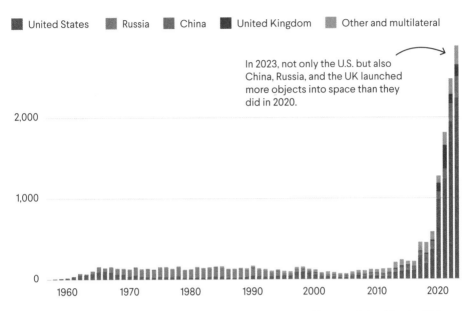

In 2023, not only the U.S. but also China, Russia, and the UK launched more objects into space than they did in 2020.

Note: Data reflects the commissioning country (i.e., the country making use of the object), which may differ from the country carrying out the launch. Data for Russia includes the Soviet Union.

Source: UN Office for Outer Space Affairs.

objects launched into space quadrupled from 2019 to 2023.[6] The number of objects launched from the United States increased nearly six times in those four years. SpaceX accounts for most of that dramatic expansion, which includes the company's contracts with the U.S. Department of Defense and NASA (see figure 2). SpaceX's Starlink satellite constellation accounts for some 60 percent of all satellites in space.

This Task Force Report focuses primarily on LEO, an altitude up to 1,243 miles. Satellites also orbit in medium Earth orbit (MEO), 1,243 miles to 22,236 miles, and geosynchronous orbit (GEO), above 22,236 miles (see figure 3).[7] However, the launch of megaconstellations and other commercial activities has increased congestion at lower altitudes, hence this report's focus on LEO. Access to desirable locations within LEO is a limited and increasingly scarce resource. The barriers to entry are low and getting lower as prices drop. According to Thomas G. Roberts at the Center for Strategic and International Studies Aerospace

Figure 2

Driven by SpaceX, U.S. Commercial Space Launches Have Taken Off
Commercial space launches for U.S. companies

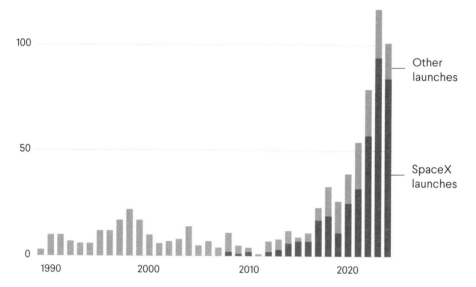

Notes: Includes launches licensed with the Federal Aviation Administration. Data for 2024 is as of September 5.

Source: Federal Aviation Administration.

Security Project, twenty years ago, the cost of a launch to LEO was $8,100/kg on an Atlas V rocket and $10,400/kg on a Delta IV rocket. In 2010, the Falcon 9 brought that cost down to $2,600/kg.[8]

Adding to the congestion is the rise in space debris, driven significantly by three recent events. In 2007, an ASAT test that China conducted against one of its own weather satellites created more than three thousand pieces of trackable debris. Two years later, Cosmos 2251, an inactive Russian satellite, collided with an Iridium satellite, creating over two thousand pieces of debris.[9] In November 2021, Russia conducted a direct-ascent ASAT missile test against one of its own satellites, creating thousands of pieces of debris.[10] That action even endangered its own citizens, as Russian cosmonauts as well as the U.S. and European astronauts working on the ISS were ordered to shelter in the attached emergency escape vehicles due to the risk of debris collision.[11] The increase in congestion and space debris makes those types of collisions more likely. That endangers not just assets such as satellites

Figure 3

Types of Orbits

Geosynchronous Orbit (GEO)
Geosynchronous orbit allows a satellite to stay "fixed" above the same point on Earth, a useful feature for observation. Because GEO requires a precise altitude, this thin shell of space is relatively crowded, despite having fewer than one thousand satellites.

Medium Earth Orbit (MEO)
Medium Earth orbit is the largest and least crowded space. It is home to the fewest satellites, though notably includes the GPS constellation.

Low Earth Orbit (LEO)
Low Earth orbit is home to thousands of satellites, far more than MEO or GEO. The relatively crowded space includes Starlink, the International Space Station, and many others. The proximity to Earth affords multiple advantages, including easier transportation and lower costs.

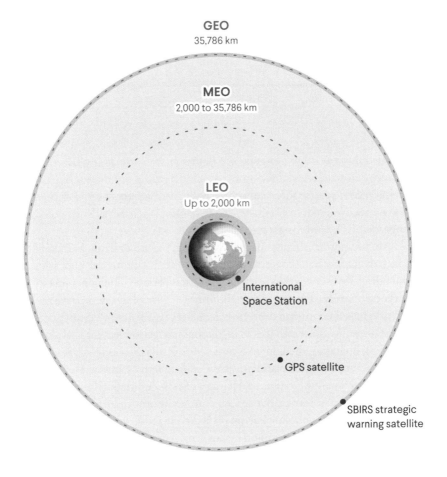

GEO
35,786 km

MEO
2,000 to 35,786 km

LEO
Up to 2,000 km

International
Space Station

GPS satellite

SBIRS strategic
warning satellite

Figure 4

Collisions and Weapons Tests Have Caused Massive Increases in Orbital Debris

Number of objects in Earth's orbit

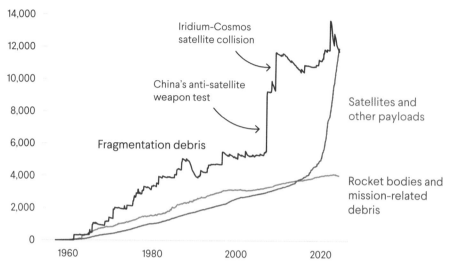

Source: NASA.

but also the lives of astronauts (see figure 4). As early as 1978, NASA scientist Donald Kessler foresaw that an increasing number of objects in space could cause more collisions, which would create more debris, and hence even more collisions. The cascading "Kessler Effect" would degrade LEO, rendering it uneconomic.

Even as services from space have become more endangered, daily life has increasingly come to depend on them. Billions of people—including farmers growing crops, businesspeople managing inventory, and parents dressing their children for school—rely on weather reports based on information from satellites (see figure 5). As of 2021, there were 6.5 billion devices using global navigation satellite systems (GNSS), including the United States' GPS, Russia's GLONASS, China's BeiDou, the European Union's Galileo, India's Indian Regional Navigation Satellite System, and Japan's Quasi-Zenith Satellite System (see figure 6). Moreover, the space economy is only growing. In April 2024, the World Economic Forum projected that the global space economy "will be worth $1.8 trillion by 2035, up from $630 billion in 2023," expanding at "almost twice the rate of global GDP growth."[12] The space

Figure 5

How Satellites Work

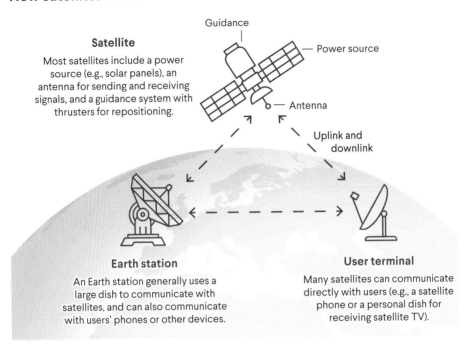

Satellite

Guidance

Power source

Most satellites include a power source (e.g., solar panels), an antenna for sending and receiving signals, and a guidance system with thrusters for repositioning.

Antenna

Uplink and downlink

Earth station

An Earth station generally uses a large dish to communicate with satellites, and can also communicate with users' phones or other devices.

User terminal

Many satellites can communicate directly with users (e.g., a satellite phone or a personal dish for receiving satellite TV).

economy encompasses not only satellites and launch vehicles, but other activities such as spacecraft servicing and repair, weather prediction, and Earth imagery analysis.

The international institutions that touch space issues were intended to support the exchange of minimum amounts of basic information among a small number of governments, not to manage a dynamic space economy. During the Cold War, neither the United States nor the Soviet Union wanted such organizations to meddle in their superpower competition. The presumption was that only a handful of governments would have space programs. In the 1960s and 1970s, the UN Committee on the Peaceful Uses of Outer Space (COPUOS) provided a useful forum for the negotiation of the four major space treaties dealing with outer space principles, rescue and return, liability, and spacecraft registration. Those remain the foundation of space governance. However, as the treaties became more specific and space politics changed, fewer states ratified them. The fifth, known as the 1979 Moon Treaty, has never been adopted by any of the major space powers.[13]

Figure 6

Satellite Constellations

A constellation is a network of satellites that work together, with orbital paths coordinated to allow continuous coverage for most points on Earth.

Constellations can be small or large: GPS is a constellation of twenty-four satellites, while Starlink is a megaconstellation of thousands.

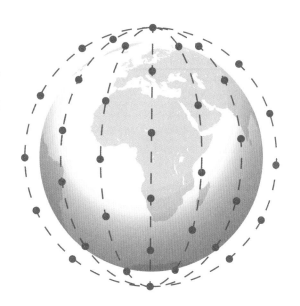

For the United States, space has been a realm for both scientific exploration and national security competition. Led by NASA, the United States has accomplished a series of extraordinary feats, including being the first country to send human beings to and from the Moon and operating the James Webb Space Telescope to study the history of the universe. In 2019, the United States created a new military service, the Space Force, to enhance national security, bringing together organizations previously located across different branches of the military.

The United States has also expanded its space diplomacy. The Principles for Cooperation in the Civil Exploration and Use of the Moon, Mars, Comets, and Asteroids for Peaceful Purposes, better known as the Artemis Accords, which the first Donald Trump administration initiated in late 2020 with eight signatories, dramatically expanded under the Joe Biden administration. In 2024, more countries joined, bringing the total number of signatories to fifty-two by the end of the year.

Space traffic management is needed to preserve the value of space. "Management" connotes the intentional allocation of assets and resources to implement a strategy. The principal reason for the need for international space traffic management is increasing congestion in LEO. Access to desirable locations within LEO will become a scarce resource. Currently, states assign LEO orbital positions when granting a license to launch, but that is a national process. There is currently no dedicated international mechanism to deconflict overlapping allocations. Unlike geostationary orbit, a type of geosynchronous orbit where satellites in effect orbit over a fixed spot, coordination of locations in LEO is more difficult.

The stakes are high. Russia's debris-causing ASAT tests and its willingness to challenge norms endanger the peaceful use of space for everyone. China's emergence as a peer competitor in space makes U.S. strategic planning for this domain more difficult and more urgent. Without immediate changes to how space is governed, the benefits of access to space could be lost to everyone. As the leading spacefaring country and the home base of the most innovative space companies, the United States is uniquely positioned to determine this future.

FINDINGS

1. U.S. leadership in space is critical to U.S. national security, to U.S. global leadership, to U.S. hard and soft power, and to the security and prosperity of the American people.

Geopolitical competition in space is heating up. After a long, post–Cold War lull, the United States' command of the commons is once again contested. Whether in the South China Sea or in the thawing Arctic, superpowers, great powers, and middle powers seek to have a say in the governance of the global commons. Not surprisingly, that competition is now extending to space, the next big domain for human activity. U.S. leadership in space will increasingly be a vital component of maintaining U.S. leadership on Earth.

Space activity can be divided into three categories: civil, national security, and commercial. Civil space activities include the iconic feats of scientific exploration that have taken place since the 1950s, largely led by NASA. Those accomplishments engender soft power emanating from space-inspired respect and goodwill. National security activities include surveilling the globe and monitoring compliance with arms-control agreements. The United States, for its part, has satellites in GEO that provide warning and assessments of a strategic nuclear attack on its territory, as well as space assets in LEO that are critical to U.S. military operations. Commercial space activities, the newest category, include companies providing launch services or information based on Earth observation. The U.S. economy is increasingly dependent on networks of commercial satellites launched by a subset of private companies: notably SpaceX and Amazon's forthcoming Project Kuiper (see figure 7).

Figure 7

The Starlink Megaconstellation Is Enormous

A subsidiary of Elon Musk's SpaceX, Starlink is a satellite internet company that provides broadband internet access in over 100 countries.

As of September 2024, Starlink consists of over **6,000 satellites**, representing the majority of active satellites orbiting Earth. SpaceX plans to expand to at least 12,000. Known as a megaconstellation, the satellites form a network around Earth, using lasers to coordinate with one another.

Ukraine has relied on Starlink in its war with Russia, placing SpaceX and Elon Musk at the center of a geopolitical flashpoint.

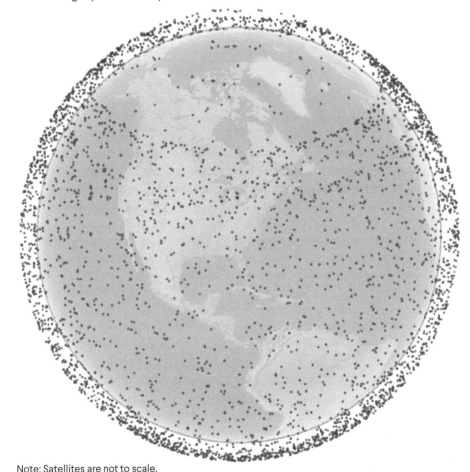

Note: Satellites are not to scale.

Source: CelesTrak.

2. Space traffic management is crucial to the well-being of modern human societies. Actions taken—or not taken—now will shape human activity in space for decades. Without changes in how humans use space, the benefits of access to space could be lost to everyone.

Concern about space congestion is not new, but the increasing number of objects in space is causing alarm. As Kessler predicted in 1978, the rising number of objects in space could cause a cascading cycle of increased collisions and debris creation. Half a century later, the challenge of the Kessler Effect is even more real.

When speaking at the Space Symposium on April 9, 2024, NASA Deputy Administrator Pamela Melroy described a close call:

> Let me tell you what: this time was really different. It was very shocking, personally, and also for all of us at NASA. On February 28, at 1:30 in the morning, a NASA spacecraft called "TIMED," and a Russian satellite—neither of them maneuverable—were expected to make a close pass to one another. Not kilometers apart. We recently learned through analysis that the pass ended up being less than ten meters apart. Within the hard-body parameters of both satellites. Less than the distance of me to the front row. Had the two satellites collided, we would have seen significant debris generation.[14]

Even when operators of spacecraft want to pass each other safely and avoid collision, there are not established rules of who passes whom and how. Bringing together countries and companies to set such rules would be a practical step toward better space governance.

3. U.S. space assets are increasingly vulnerable to attacks by China, Russia, and other potential adversaries—attacks that could come from the ground, the air, or space itself.

The United States leads the world in the number of operational satellites, a portfolio that includes many large, sophisticated, "exquisite" satellites in GEO with unique arms-control verification, nuclear attack warning, and intelligence capabilities. Those national security and commercial space assets are increasingly vulnerable. China and Russia have developed the means to divert, disable, or destroy those assets through a diverse set of capabilities, including electronic warfare and jamming, direct-ascent ASAT missiles, directed energy systems such as ground-based lasers, and potential developments such as space-based kinetic weapons and orbiting space robots that could attack adversaries' satellites.[15] In recent years, the United States has begun to deploy a larger number of smaller assets in other orbits to distribute the risk. Even so, U.S. efforts to counter the vulnerability of its satellites have not kept up with the threat.

China and Russia pose different types of threats to strategic stability in space. Russia's actions endanger satellites in space now, while China's plans not only threaten space assets, but also challenge the United States' future leadership in space. This section focuses on Russia, the next on China.

Russia's November 2021 ASAT test against its own satellite was an ominous sign. Worrisome threats continue to come from Russia. The country already has interfered with a space asset for military reasons. Just before its 2022 invasion of Ukraine, a Russian cyberattack disabled terminals for Viasat, a U.S. company on contract to provide satellite communications to Ukraine. As the attack made clear, space and cyberspace are interdependent. Global information technology infrastructure is becoming more dependent on space systems with companies such as Amazon, SpaceX, and others building global space-based 5G backplanes that will serve communication and information processing needs worldwide. As a result, space systems that comprise segments of those infrastructures have become cyber targets. In the words of a report by the American Institute of Aeronautics and Astronautics, "...the transnational nature of space operations makes the cybersecurity of space systems a matter that should be of common interest to all countries."[16]

Moscow seems intent on gaining the ability to disrupt key U.S. capabilities, including communications, GPS, early warning, intelligence, and command and control. In May 2024, then Assistant Secretary of Defense for Space Policy John F. Plumb testified to Congress that Moscow is "developing a concerning anti-satellite capability," including "electronic warfare, directed energy weapons, direct-ascent anti-satellite systems, and orbital systems with counterspace applications." Those investments, he went on to explain, "are designed to exploit what it views as a U.S. overreliance on space for conducting military operations and to offset perceived U.S. military advantages."[17]

Even more concerning is Russia's possible intention to deploy a nuclear weapon in space, which would pose a catastrophic threat to satellites, particularly those also orbiting in LEO. U.S. officials have warned of that threat.

Although current international treaties prohibit governments from placing nuclear weapons in space, U.S. adversaries have moved increasingly closer to breaking international norms on Earth and in orbit. Putting a nuclear weapon in space would be a dangerous escalation and would violate two important international treaties. Such a weapon could be used to create an electromagnetic pulse and disable many satellites, or worse. It would also violate the 1963 Limited Test Ban Treaty, which the United States and the Soviet Union (and other countries) signed after the United States' disastrous "Starfish Prime" nuclear test in 1962. Detonated 250 miles above Earth, that test not only caused an electrical blackout 900 miles away in Hawaii but also knocked out Telstar 1, a communications satellite launched by NASA months earlier.

Sending a nuclear weapon into space would also violate the 1967 Outer Space Treaty, an agreement ratified by spacefaring powers with nuclear weapons—China, France, Russia, the United Kingdom, and the United States—and 110 other countries. As Article IV of the treaty states:

> States Parties to the Treaty undertake not to place in orbit around the earth any objects carrying nuclear weapons or any other kinds of weapons of mass destruction, install such weapons on celestial bodies, or station such weapons in outer space in any other manner.
>
> The moon and other celestial bodies shall be used by all States Parties to the Treaty exclusively for peaceful purposes. The establishment of military bases, installations and fortifications, the testing of any type of weapons and the conduct of military maneuvers on celestial bodies shall be forbidden. The use of military personnel for scientific research or for any other peaceful purposes shall not be prohibited. The use of any equipment or facility necessary for peaceful exploration of the moon and other celestial bodies shall also not be prohibited.[18]

The United States is not the only country concerned about Russia's intentions, which would contravene the text of the Outer Space Treaty. According to then Assistant Secretary of State for Arms Control, Deterrence, and Stability Mallory Stewart, the U.S. government has discussed Russia's plans with China and India.[19] Familiar geostrategic rifts are evident. The United States' claims of Russian plans to weaponize space led to debates in the UN Security Council. In April 2024, the UN Security Council considered a resolution that was sponsored by the United States and Japan and called for "all States, in particular those with major space capabilities, to contribute actively to the objective of the peaceful use of outer space and of the prevention of an arms race in outer space."[20] Thirteen of the fifteen Security Council members approved. China abstained, while Russia vetoed the resolution. In December 2024, the UN General Assembly voted 167 to 4 to adopt a resolution on "prevention of an arms race in outer space."[21] Again, Russia voted no, and China abstained.[22] As there is no veto in the General Assembly, the measure passed.

4. While the United States remains the leading space power across the civil, commercial, and national security realms, China is emerging as a peer competitor.

China could soon reach its goal to overtake the United States as the leading space power. In a declassified 2021 report, the Office of the Director of National Intelligence assesses that "China is steadily progressing toward its goal of becoming a world-class space leader with the intent to match or exceed the United States by 2045. Even by 2030, China probably will achieve world-class status in all but a few space technology areas." The report further states that "by 2030 Chinese space activities will increasingly erode the national security, commercial, and global influence advantage that the United States has accrued from its leadership in space."[23]

In the past five years, China has launched over five hundred objects into space, built its own orbiting space station, and placed two landers on the far side of the Moon.[24] As Major General Greg Gagnon, the deputy chief of space operations for intelligence in the U.S. Space Force, put it in May 2024, the country "has rapidly advanced in space in a way that few people can appreciate."[25] In 2021, China began construction on its Tiangong space station, which, although much smaller than the ISS, could be expanded.[26] The ISS, for its part, will be retired by 2030. NASA is looking to commercial space stations to meet its needs beyond then, freeing up agency resources for more ambitious exploration goals. NASA's decision is indicative of its changing priorities, fostered by scarce financial resources.

China is building space capabilities for military use. In its 2023 report *Military and Security Developments Involving the People's Republic of China*, the U.S. Department of Defense stated, "The PLA [People's Liberation Army] views space superiority, the ability to control the space-enabled information sphere and to deny adversaries their own space-based information gathering and communication capabilities, as critical components to conduct modern 'informatized warfare.'"[27] The United States relies heavily on space-based assets for surveillance and weapons guidance, making it especially wary of adversaries' capabilities to deny access to those assets. In the previously cited May 1, 2024, congressional testimony, Plumb went on to describe China's capabilities, including "electronic warfare, direct-ascent anti-satellite (ASAT) missiles, directed-energy systems such as ground-based lasers, potential space-based kinetic weapons, and orbiting space robots," which could "hold our on-orbit assets at risk."[28]

Unsurprisingly, China has made space a prominent part of its grand strategy. The country's New Strategic Frontiers policy, which began over a decade ago, includes space, polar, sea, and cyberspace, areas Chinese officials appear to see as ungoverned spaces.[29] In the same vein, China's thirteenth Five-Year Plan, released in 2016, promised that the country would take "an active role in formulating international rules in areas such as the internet, the deep sea, the polar regions, and space."[30]

China even has its own form of a growing commercial space sector. The China Satellite Network Group is in the process of launching the Guowang constellation of thirteen thousand satellites—its answer to Starlink. As of February 2024, Shanghai Spacecom Satellite Technology had raised $943 million for its projected G60 constellation of twelve thousand satellites, another Starlink-like endeavor.[31] In August 2024, the China Aerospace Science and Technology Corporation, the largest state-owned contractor, launched into orbit the project's first eighteen satellites. Like China's advances in electric vehicles, the country's commercial space sector benefits from heavy government investment in new technology. Furthermore, to some observers, China's collection of soil samples suggests not only scientific exploration but also possible plans to mine the Moon.[32]

In an era of competition, dual-use technologies take on added significance. China has invested in a robotic arm to grab space debris, but this tool is capable of completing not only a civil clean up task but also a military mission to disable an adversary's satellite. China has already demonstrated its ability to wield the arm for the more sinister scenario, using it to move a defunct Beidou satellite out of its operational orbit.

China is also making space a part of its strategy toward the Global South. The Space Information Corridor, a component of its Belt and Road Initiative, connects countries to Beidou's GNSS services. In a similar way, China's leadership of the Asia Pacific Space Cooperation

Figure 8

Low Earth Orbit Is a Free-for-All

Density of satellites and debris by altitude (wider bars mean more objects orbiting at that altitude)

● Active satellites   ● Debris and inactive objects (approximate distribution)

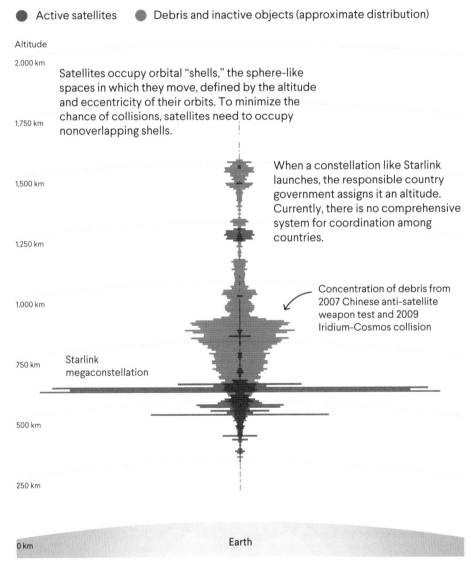

Altitude

2,000 km

Satellites occupy orbital "shells," the sphere-like spaces in which they move, defined by the altitude and eccentricity of their orbits. To minimize the chance of collisions, satellites need to occupy nonoverlapping shells.

1,750 km

1,500 km

When a constellation like Starlink launches, the responsible country government assigns it an altitude. Currently, there is no comprehensive system for coordination among countries.

1,250 km

Concentration of debris from 2007 Chinese anti-satellite weapon test and 2009 Iridium-Cosmos collision

1,000 km

750 km   Starlink megaconstellation

500 km

250 km

0 km   Earth

Note: Altitudes of orbits are approximate. Most objects have elliptical orbits, meaning their altitude varies as they orbit Earth. The altitude used is the perigee (lowest point of orbit).

Source: Jonathan McDowell, General Catalog of Artificial Space Objects.

Organization, which promotes collaborative space programs, gives it soft power advantages across developing countries.

Competition between the United States and China is evident in other types of space exploration. Just as certain spots on Earth provide strategic advantage, favorable orbital positions will be contested (see figure 8). Examples include areas in Earth and lunar orbit called "Lagrange points." Named for the mathematician Joseph-Louis Lagrange, those desirable positions in space occur, as NASA has explained, "where the gravitational forces of a two-body system like the Sun and the Earth produce enhanced regions of attraction and repulsion."[33] Held in place by gravity from two different bodies, spacecraft positioned at such points need less fuel to remain stationary. NASA's James Webb Space Telescope, for instance, gazes into outer space from L2, the Lagrange point on the far side of the Moon. China's Queqiao communications relay satellite sits near that same point and communicated with the Chang'e 4 lander when it made its historic touchdown on the far side of the Moon in 2019.

Although China is the pressing challenge, U.S. policymakers should remember that not all competition in space raises geostrategic enmity. Even non-adversarial countries see space programs as a mark of great power status. Indian authorities have noted that they want to be included in making the decisions regarding use of the Moon. Being technologically advanced helps states be part of the "in" group setting international rules. Strategists recall that already-existing nuclear powers gained a special status under the Treaty on the Nonproliferation of Nuclear Weapons.[34] Having successfully landed a device near the lunar south pole, India stakes its claim to be part of whatever system will govern lunar affairs in the future. In 2023, India signed the Artemis Accords.

5. Current international organizations and treaties are ill suited to the new realities of space activity, and no single multilateral body is designed to comprehensively manage space traffic.

Unlike aviation, shipping, and telecommunications, the space economy lacks a unified, single international institution that can establish or enforce an agreed-on set of best practices. Other domains boast international organizations that can issue legally binding rules based on treaties that governments have ratified. Aviation has the International Civil Aviation Organization (ICAO). Ocean shipping has the International Maritime Organization (IMO). Telecommunications has the ITU.

Figure 9

Space Issues Fall Under Multiple UN Agencies

UN bodies that address some aspect of outer space policy

UN General Assembly (UNGA)

→ **First Committee (Disarmament and International Security)**
Supported by the Conference on Disarmament, the First Committee's focus includes the militarization of space, among other issues.

→ **Fourth Committee (Special Political and Decolonization)**
↓
Committee on the Peaceful Uses of Outer Space (COPUOS)
COPUOS is the UN's dedicated forum for cooperation around outer space issues, and has 102 member states. It is supported by the Office for Outer Space Affairs (UNOOSA), and convenes the Scientific and Technical Subcommittee and the Legal Subcommittee.

UN Economic and Social Council (ECOSOC)

→ Of the many specialized agencies under ECOSOC, four have remits that include some aspect of space policy:

International Civil Aviation Organization (ICAO)

International Maritime Organization (IMO)

International Telecommunications Union (ITU)

World Meteorological Organization (WMO)

These four specialized agencies also inform the work of UNGA.

Source: United Nations.

Space issues, by contrast, come under the remit of three different UN bodies (see figure 9):

- COPUOS, based in Vienna, has a broad mandate to discuss developments in space. Among its actions, it promotes sharing of space-related information among its members, which helps disseminate best practices. COPUOS is supported by UNOOSA, an office of the UN Secretariat, and reports to the UN General Assembly through the

Fourth Committee, which handles special political and decolonization issues.

- The ITU, based in Geneva, is a specialized agency that allocates frequencies and orbital positions for satellites in GEO and frequencies for satellites in LEO. Every three to four years, it holds the World Radiocommunication Conference (WRC), where its members agree to policies and programs to update telecommunications.[35] The 2027 iteration of the conference is slated to consider communications on the Moon, the growth of the satellites sector, and space weather (solar phenomena, such as a burst of radiation, can create space weather that interferes with satellite communications near Earth). ITU Secretary-General Doreen Bogdan-Martin has estimated that 80 percent of the agenda will be space-related.[36]

- The Conference on Disarmament (CD) is a third UN body ostensibly responsible for space. The CD was supposed to address the demilitarization of space, among other duties. But the CD's work has been deadlocked for years, stalled by disputes unrelated to space.

Some of the various institutions responsible for space have made efforts to cooperate with one another. In 2015, 2016, and 2017, for example, UNOOSA and ICAO held a joint Aerospace Symposium.[37] At the sixty-seventh session of COPUOS, in June 2024, an IMO representative gave a presentation on "marine environmental effects of jettisoned waste from commercial spaceflight activities."[38] This topic previews a coming issue: heightened concern about the effects on marine life and conditions of the practice of deorbiting spacecraft by crashing them into Earth's oceans.

Outside formal institutions, the United States cooperates on space directly with its allies and partners. In September 2024, the Combined Space Operations Initiative, a diplomatic grouping of U.S. allies, marked its tenth anniversary of "cooperation and coordination of national security space activities." The group now counts nine countries in addition to the United States: Australia, Canada, France, Germany, Italy, Japan, New Zealand, Norway, and the United Kingdom.[39] The same year, General Chance Saltzman, the highest-ranking officer in the U.S. Space Force, added an officer from an allied country to his leadership team: UK Air Marshal Paul Godfrey, who serves as assistant chief of space operations for future concepts and partnerships.

Figure 10

Three Countries Are Responsible for Nearly All Space Junk

Spent rocket bodies and debris as of June 2024

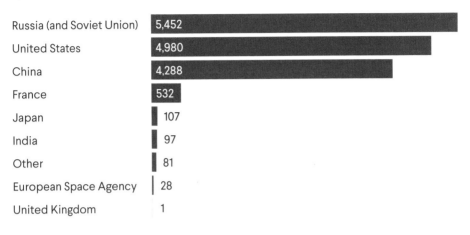

Russia (and Soviet Union)	5,452
United States	4,980
China	4,288
France	532
Japan	107
India	97
Other	81
European Space Agency	28
United Kingdom	1

Source: NASA.

In past decades, the superpowers did not want a powerful body managing space. Therefore, neither the UN system nor any other multilateral body is configured to deal comprehensively with space issues. Nor is there any international agency for managing space traffic or removing space debris. China, Russia, and the United States are the source of most of this debris, but they are also at the greatest risk from it as the three countries with the most assets in space (see figure 10).

Further complicating matters, geopolitical divisions are already characterizing the emerging institutional architecture.[40] For example, the United States and its partners have developed the Artemis Accords. Meanwhile, China has promoted its International Lunar Research Station program. So far, countries have joined one program or the other. However, with its signature of the Artemis Accords in December 2024, Thailand became the first country to join both programs. If more countries eventually join both, it could say just as much about geopolitics on Earth as about exploration in space. A country that joins both programs might want to be seen as independent or friendly to both sides (see figure 11).

Figure 11

Space Cooperation Breaks Down Along Geopolitical Lines

Participation in the U.S.-led Artemis Accords and the China- and Russia-led International Lunar Research Station (ILRS) as of December 20, 2024

■ Artemis Accords signatory　■ ILRS participant　■ Participant in both

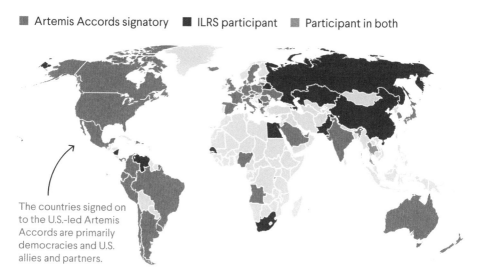

The countries signed on to the U.S.-led Artemis Accords are primarily democracies and U.S. allies and partners.

Sources: U.S. State Department; CFR research.

6. The expertise and perspective of the private sector and other non-state actors is critical to effective space traffic management.

Expert input from the private sector is necessary to shape effective rules of the road for space traffic management. The space economy is powered by innovation in the private sector. Private companies have combined technological advances with efficient managerial practices to expand the space sector. The private sector understands how proposed rules would actually affect operations. Without their constructive input, rules and regulations adopted by policymakers risk being ineffective or—even worse—deleterious to the responsible use of space. Like commercial uses of cyberspace, the outer space economy aims to combine expertise and efficiency. However, current governance mechanisms are the responsibility of states.

7. In an era of increased competition in space, the United States may not always be the first to reach new destinations in space. Therefore, the United States benefits from the principle in the Outer Space Treaty that outer space "is not subject to national appropriation by claim of sovereignty."

Commercial leaders and some policymakers assume that the United States will always benefit from a so-called first come, first claim approach. In an era of space competition, however, the United States may not always be first. Denial of ownership of space by any person, company, or government (and rejection of a first come, first claim approach) would help ensure the use of space by the United States, other countries, and populations worldwide—and would hedge against the possibility that in some areas of space (and celestial bodies), the United States might not be first to arrive or stake a claim.

The ability of more countries to reach the Moon has raised concerns among some governments and companies about the intentions of other spacefarers. Governments have not made claims but are considering use of materials found on the Moon. Although China landed a device on the far side of the Moon, it does not own the soil there. Although India landed a device on the lunar south pole, it does not own the ice that may be found there. That said, in 2015, the United States opened a path to owning and selling certain space resources by passing the Commercial Space Launch Competitiveness Act of 2015, which states that working through the federal agencies, the president

> shall promote the right of United States citizens to engage in commercial exploration for and commercial recovery of space resources free from harmful interference, in accordance with the international obligations of the United States and subject to authorization and continuing supervision by the Federal Government.[41]

In the same legislation, the United States also explains that it is "the sense of Congress that by the enactment of this Act, the United States does not thereby assert sovereignty or sovereign or exclusive rights or jurisdiction over, or the ownership of any celestial body."[42] The legislation sought to achieve a delicate balance among principles.

RECOMMENDATIONS

1. Make space a top national priority.

The U.S. president should demonstrate this commitment by convening a space summit in the first year of his administration and reassessing priorities to include whether to declare key space systems to be "critical infrastructure." At a space summit, the United States should bring together signatories of the Artemis Accords, leading space companies, scientists, and other participants to reinforce the United States as the foremost spacefaring country. These efforts could emphasize the Trump administration's commitment to secure space for national defense and global stability by protecting and enhancing U.S. assets in space, ground control centers, launch locations, and receiver nodes.

Regarding critical infrastructure, the Trump administration should bring together industry, experts, and policymakers to address this issue. An April 2024 National Security Memorandum stated, "Critical infrastructure comprises the physical and virtual assets and systems so vital to the Nation that their incapacity or destruction would have a debilitating impact on national security, national economic security, or national public health or safety."[43] But despite the recommendation of the Department of Homeland Security, space was not included among the sixteen sectors deemed "critical" in the Biden administration's 2024 policy review.[44]

A critical infrastructure designation for space systems would convey immediate benefits. It would signal to the United States, its allies and partners, and the greater international community a commitment to defending the space sector. It would provide—through a sector risk management agency—a unified point of contact within the government to coordinate with industry information regarding threats, events that endanger infrastructure, best practices in protecting infrastructure, and lessons learned from successful recovery and mitigation of such incidents. Other critical infrastructure already enjoys those benefits, which are useful for preventing incidents as well as managing and recovering from them when they do occur. The concept of "sector risk management" implies risk management throughout the entire risk life cycle of an infrastructure asset, from risk analysis and risk preparation to incident management and recovery. Applied to the space systems sector, such an approach would also provide standards for the accuracy, timeliness, and utility of information shared to protect the space systems sector.

The Department of Homeland Security's Cybersecurity and Infrastructure Security Agency, which is responsible for protecting government infrastructure, should work with NASA and the Department of Defense to implement the declaration and to identify potential gaps in the defense of the space sector.

2. Revitalize American international leadership in space.

The president should instruct relevant cabinet officers that the United States must lead the world in space. The National Security Council is well placed to support the president and to guide the interdepartmental aspects of the revitalized national effort to lead in space. The first Trump administration revived the National Space Council, which could contribute focused expertise to this campaign. Declaring space assets critical infrastructure would be a strong step, but it is not enough, because a designation does not bring additional resources.[45] The president should therefore ask the Office of Management and Budget to inventory all civil, commercial, and defense space activities funded by the federal government and propose increases in the administration's budget request. The goal is not only more money in appropriations, but also a more comprehensive and integrated approach to space policy across the federal government.

A real commitment to making space a top national priority would include additional appropriations for NASA and for the National Oceanic and Atmospheric Administration (NOAA) and its parent organization, the Department of Commerce, which is expected to take over civilian space traffic management duties from the Department of Defense. For decades, the U.S. military has used its equipment and expertise to provide a global good of warning spacefarers of potential collisions so that they could maneuver apart. As part of a multiyear transition, this service will be transferred to a civilian agency, the Department of Commerce. This change is emblematic of the rise of the commercial space economy; increasingly, the users of this service are space companies. In September 2024, the Department of Commerce announced that NOAA had begun the initial trial phase of the Traffic Coordination System for Space (known as TraCSS).[46] In addition, the U.S. Congress could use legislation to reinforce this transfer of duties, an idea that has spanned administrations.

3. Fix the vulnerability problem and enhance deterrence.

In space, the advantage favors offense. As the political scientist Forrest E. Morgan explains, "orbital space is an offense dominant environment—that is to say, it is easier to attack satellites and their supporting infrastructure than it is to defend those assets."[47] Therefore, strategists need to develop measures to deter potential adversaries from attacking a vulnerable asset in the first place. One approach is deterrence by punishment—to make a credible promise of a powerful reprisal for an attack. Another is deterrence by denial—to make it difficult for the potential attacker to obtain its desired objective. Larger constellations and proliferated satellites change the calculations of potential attackers by reducing the offensive advantage.

The president should launch a space vulnerability, remediation, and deterrence assessment that includes participation by the Department of Defense, the intelligence community, the U.S. Space Force, private sector space companies, and representatives of civil space organizations and academic institutions. This type of interdepartmental cooperation that includes experts outside the government is itself an innovation in space policy. Such an integrated approach would reflect the United States' prioritization of space policy.

The assessment team should produce recommendations for remediating vulnerability deficiencies and enhancing capabilities across the full range of potential defensive measures, including: enhancing domain awareness; proliferating and widely distributing space assets in order to increase their resiliency; hardening space assets against various modes of attack; providing space assets with defensive capabilities; and developing on-demand replacement assets that can be deployed quickly in the event that the initial set of space assets have been disabled or destroyed.

The assessment team should also develop recommendations for enhancing deterrence in order to discourage attacks on space assets by both state and nonstate actors. These efforts should include branding any effort to put nuclear weapons in space as a violation of the 1967 Outer Space Treaty (signed by China, Russia, and over 112 other nations) and seeking international agreement to ban destructive ASAT tests (like those conducted by China and Russia).

The United States should continue to focus on deepening norms against ASAT testing. Motivated by Russia's aforementioned November 2021 ASAT test that destroyed its own satellite and spewed debris, the United States led a coordinated response. In a formal declaration on April 18, 2022, the United States committed to not conduct destructive direct-ascent ASAT testing and urged other countries to do the same.[48] This policy applies to ASAT devices launched from the ground into space with the intent of destroying another satellite. This category does not include ASAT measures launched from within space. The United States also championed the 2022 UN General Assembly resolution A/RES/77/41 that called for states not to perform direct-ascent ASAT testing.[49] The measure was adopted by a vote of 155 in favor, with 9 opposed (including China and Russia) and 9 abstaining.[50] That resolution called on countries to "develop further practical steps," including "additional moratoriums."[51] For example, the United States and other countries should extend the commitment to include forbearance from launching destructive ASAT tests from within space as well.

4. Sharpen policy on China and seek strategic engagement on hotline issues.

Even though the United States will need to act unilaterally to deter dangerous actions by China, Washington can make long-term bilateral moves that would improve safety in space. Even as it competes with China in space, the U.S. government should conduct a targeted, space-related engagement with the country on "hotline" communications, space traffic management, and the rescue of spacefarers in distress. With an increasing number of spacecraft and people going into space, the two countries share an interest in rescue, space traffic management, and space debris mitigation; after all, neither wants to collide unintentionally.

The United States and China should develop principles, consultative mechanisms, data exchanges, and hotline communication channels, all in an effort to reduce risks and de-escalate potential confrontations in space. This engagement would resemble the channel of communication the United States had with the Soviet Union during the Cold War and would be in the United States' interest.

The United States and China also share an interest in managing space traffic, an issue that is only becoming more complicated. If plans succeed, Starlink will be joined by other satellite constellations, such as Amazon's Project Kuiper, in a few years. Chinese entities plan to launch their own megaconstellations, such as the G60, on a similar time frame. As the home bases of megaconstellations, both the United States and China need to agree on common rules for space traffic management. Countries can have deep rivalries but adhere to practical international rules, as in civilian air traffic. Both China and the United States want to be sure that their airliners can land safely at each other's airports.

Rescue is another area ripe for cooperation. In the harsh realm beyond Earth, rival crews could find that they need each other if caught in dire circumstances. To that end, one option includes updating the Rescue Agreement. Signed in 1968 as an elaboration of the Outer Space Treaty, the agreement builds on one of the oldest concepts in modern international law, the idea of rescue at sea, and is now ratified by the United States, China, and Russia, as well as ninety-seven other countries. The United States and China need not spearhead the effort. A more viable approach would be for both to support another country's diplomatic leadership. Negotiators should expand the Rescue Agreement beyond its current focus on assisting astronauts who have returned to Earth in distress so that the agreement also covers search and rescue for astronauts who are still in orbit or on the Moon. As people travel deeper into space, the need for extra safety measures grows. Moreover, as commercial space traffic increases, there will be an increasing need for medical care, as not everyone in space will be a physically fit astronaut. Especially beyond Earth orbit, it would not be possible to return home quickly for medical procedures. Instead, that care would need to be administered while in space. The expanding field of space medicine will likely need to borrow lessons from emergency health care in other extreme environments, such as undersea or wilderness medicine.

To proceed with these practical actions, the United States will need to update and refine the Wolf Amendment, a provision that has been included in annual congressional appropriations since 2011. Named for Representative Frank Wolf (R-VA), the provision restricts NASA and the White House Office of Science and Technology Policy from cooperating with China. The measure was originally created more to criticize China's human rights record than to protect national security, although it has been amended over the years as U.S. concerns about espionage have risen. Currently, if NASA scientists want to work with their Chinese counterparts, they need to notify Congress and the FBI in advance. For example, before requesting access to the soil samples China collected from the far side of the Moon in 2024, NASA had to notify Congress. Ironically, the Wolf Amendment puts the United States at a disadvantage vis-à-vis China by making it harder for U.S. scientists to access material and information that scientists in the rest of the world can easily obtain.

Another problem with the Wolf Amendment is that it reinforces China's narrative that the United States opposes international cooperation. Of course, the United States should be vigilant in its interactions with a potential adversary. But the amendment should focus on measures to prevent espionage and technology theft. It should include a carve-out for basic scientific research activities, such as communication, the sharing of scientific data, and invitations to examine samples from space. As China's role in space continues to change, the decade-old amendment should be updated for new circumstances.

As the home bases of megaconstellations, both the United States and China need to agree on common rules for space traffic management.

A more creative approach would identify new avenues for engagement that the United States and China would find beneficial. For example, the two countries could determine safe distances for activities, such as in-space servicing when a support vehicle maneuvers close to a satellite. This measure could allay mutual suspicions that those activities conceal military purposes.

Another way forward involves the concept of exchange—a powerful idea, since neither side concedes and both sides gain. During the Cold War, the United States and the Soviet Union created the Apollo-Soyuz program, which led to a historic docking in space in 1975. Borrowing from the past, the United States and China could hold a joint conference of American astronauts and Chinese taikonauts that focuses on the importance of rescue on the ground. This would serve as a starting point for cooperation between the countries, which could lead to deeper conversations addressing rescue in space, including interoperability of equipment. Additionally, the United States could suggest establishing a joint research lab, where scientists from both countries could investigate samples from the Moon.

In a more ambitious move, the United States could propose an exchange of astronauts and taikonauts, allowing each to fly on the other's space station. China would allow American astronauts to visit the Tiangong space station, and the United States would allow Chinese taikonauts to visit the ISS before its planned retirement in 2030. There is little security risk in opening up the ISS to Chinese participation: as of October 2024, NASA reports that "280 individuals representing 23 countries, and 5 International Partners have visited the International Space Station." [52] Of those, fifty-seven were Russian. Reflecting the post–Cold War era of cooperation, the ISS was intentionally built with a Russian component. Russian participation has continued despite the war in Ukraine, reinforcing the point that life-sustaining cooperation in space can transcend disagreements on Earth. A U.S.-China exchange initiative could improve civil space relations and help sustain practical cooperation on space traffic management.

5. Build on existing international regimes to improve space traffic management.

As there is no single comprehensive organization for managing space, the Task Force recommends building on existing international organizations to create a new web of cooperation. This system would be based on UNOOSA and the ITU. To that end, there are steps that the United States and other countries should take. This section begins with top priorities and then explores more detailed descriptions of the recommended bodies and structures.

Expand the Artemis Accords. Established under the first Trump administration, the Artemis Accords have over fifty signatories. To unleash the power of this set of principles governing the use of space, the State Department should further develop an Artemis Accords coordination group composed of officials and experts who work together to advance shared principles. A group of Artemis Accord countries met on the margins of the 2024 International Astronautical Congress.[53] As Michael Gold, a former associate administrator of NASA, has said: "The accords were designed to be a beginning of a discussion, not an ending. They have been tremendously effective in creating momentum for the dialog and norms of behavior in venues like the United Nations involving China and Russia."[54] The Artemis Accords advance useful principles such as interoperability, and they call on "partner nations to utilize open international standards, develop new standards when necessary, and strive to support interoperability to the greatest extent practical."[55]

Offer lessons learned about aspects of space management. The ITU could provide lessons learned from its decades of work on spectrum allocation, which could inform the deconfliction of LEO orbits and issuance of debris mitigation guidelines. The ITU already allocates frequencies and orbital positions for satellites in GEO and frequencies for satellites in LEO. The ITU could analyze which, if any, aspects of managing GEO provide insights for promoting safety in the very different setting of LEO. Currently, countries assign LEO orbital positions when granting a license to launch, but this is a national process. There is currently no dedicated international mechanism to deconflict overlapping allocations. Unlike in GEO, where geosynchronous satellites in effect stay over a fixed spot, the movement of satellites in LEO might be changed, making allocation of location difficult.

Assist spacefaring states. UNOOSA, with its power to convene groups and gather and disseminate information to COPUOS members and the public, is well placed to help states and other parties meet international standards for safe operation in space. Therefore, it should expand its resources for new spacefaring states. It can help states build their capacity for meeting standards of good practice. Furthermore, governments could be more willing to receive advice from UNOOSA, a theoretically apolitical office within the UN Secretariat, than they would directly from other governments. The United States should support the allocation of resources within the UN budget to enhance UNOOSA's capacities.

Participate actively. Neither international organizations nor more informal international regimes function well without sustained attention from their members. Active participation by the United States and its friends and allies in these international organizations will be critical to ensuring that they effectively carry out the tasks given to them. The United States is well placed to be a constructive leader. The United States should continue to take an active role in the international organizations that help manage space.

Working through existing organizations is an option, for now. Given the current geopolitical climate, it is neither politically nor economically feasible to create a new formal international organization for space, which would require negotiating and ratifying a new treaty. Future diplomats, however, may want to revisit this approach and craft a new organization to support cooperation in space.

In the meantime, policymakers should craft regimes of cooperation on space issues that use existing organizations. Some tasks involve grappling with new technology and need a small group of technical experts to confer and agree. Other tasks involve disseminating new practices or information and require an organization that can spread ideas widely, enjoys far-reaching credibility and political acceptance, and has a broad membership. Thus, different types of organizations should be used for different tasks. Functional international organizations such as ICAO, the IMO, and the World Meteorological Organization provide managerial frameworks for their specific fields of activity. If and until the world creates a new functional international organization for space management, space policy practitioners will have to make do with borrowing the best of existing organizations. Two organizations should serve as pillars: UNOOSA and the ITU.

UNOOSA already has connections with a wide range of countries in different regions of the world. The office maintains the Register of Objects Launched into Outer Space, which lists who has launched what type of craft, making the office a logical body to provide assistance to new spacefaring states. Spacefaring states should inform UNOOSA about launches from their territory. UNOOSA could act as the repository of informational materials that help new spacefaring states meet international requirements. This capacity-building would give all states a stake in space governance, which could reduce the odds that the equivalent to merchant ships' "flags of convenience" emerge in space, kicking off a race to the bottom as countries compete to offer lower standards. Smaller spacefaring states may feel they have a voice in COPUOS, which adds to the legitimacy of space governance. All states need to recognize that space governance is beneficial not just for the major spacefaring countries but also for emerging and even non-spacefaring countries. Of course, COPUOS faces challenges, since its consensus decision-making rule means any of its 102 members can block action. The flip side to the consensus rule, however, is that all states are on an equal footing, making COPUOS (and UNOOSA) broadly acceptable to a wide range of countries.

UNOOSA also benefits from the somewhat less politicized atmosphere of being based with other UN technical agencies in Vienna. That makes it easier for governments, companies, researchers, and other entities to participate effectively. Inclusion is crucial, since standards for space operations, especially regarding traffic management, need to be followed by everyone if they are to be effective. Most of the over ninety countries that own satellites in LEO are new spacefaring countries (see figure 12).[56] Providing capacity-building or facilitating the exchange of practical practices would be a classic task for a functional office such as UNOOSA. UNOOSA has taken the initiative to include private sector

Figure 12

More Countries Are Putting Objects Into Space

Number of countries or territories with at least one satellite or other object launched (or commissioned to be launched) into space*

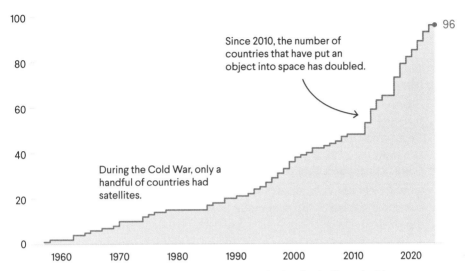

*The value for each year is the number of countries or territories that had launched (or commissioned the launch of) at least one object in that year or any previous year.

Source: UN Office for Outer Space Affairs.

speakers in gatherings such as the June 2024 Conference on Sustainable Lunar Activities, hosted by UNOOSA Director Aarti Holla-Maini. UNOOSA does not have a large staff, but it can help new spacefaring states with existing projects, as it already does with its Space Law for New Space Actors project. The project, on request, helps governments update their domestic law on space to meet international norms. At UNOOSA, member states could boost the organization's capacity (and their own influence) by loaning experts to support the international staff. Today, the United States lends one official to UNOOSA. Another innovation would be to allow member states to loan more experts up to a limit, such as five per country.

The space economy moves at the pace of innovation, and the institutions that support it need to move quickly as well. Practical structural improvements could help COPUOS support countries and companies better. For example, currently COPUOS has one two-week plenary session in June leading up to the UN General Assembly in the fall.

Many innovators in the space economy do not think COPUOS can act quickly enough to offer solutions to rapidly changing conditions in LEO, making them wary of working with this committee. Member states should increase the pace and convene plenaries twice a year. COPUOS also has two subcommittees that each meet once a year. Having these bodies meet more frequently could also help COPUOS be more responsive.

The ITU should also take on a greater role in space. The organization has a membership composed of states and is empowered to make decisions by a majority vote instead of consensus. The ITU has mechanisms to incorporate private sector expertise into its decision-making process—all of which make the ITU well placed to recommend actions that governments and other actors should take with regard to space. Already, the ITU maintains the Master International Frequency Register, which lists who has been allocated which frequency.[57] The ITU could consider new ideas, such as developing a tracking device for satellites similar to the Automatic Identification System transponder on ships.

The ITU and UNOOSA need the support of UN member states to help manage human activity in the space domain. With adequate funding and diplomatic support, these international organizations can not only draw attention to space issues but also serve as a forum in which states can craft agreements. The principal space treaties, for example, were developed in COPUOS meetings in the 1960s and 1970s.[58]

Another benefit of working through international organizations such as these is that many different member states can provide leadership on an issue; the burden does not just fall on powerful countries like the United States. In the space sector, several countries have relevant experience that can be drawn upon, while others have strong track records of bridging differences to bring states together. At a time of rising geopolitical tensions, it can be advantageous for less powerful countries to take the lead. In 2024, for example, Romania played an important role leading the successful effort to create an Action Team on Lunar Activities Consultation, which will help frame diplomatic discussions on how to manage increasing human activity on the Moon. In multilateral organizations, such groups can help define policy options that are both inventive and politically viable.[59]

Of course, the United States should make sure that new obligations do not hamper private companies' innovation in space. The United States depends on such innovation continuing in order to deliver and maintain its own advanced space capabilities. Policymakers should also make sure that any new obligations are not used by foreign actors, intentionally or not, to hamper the U.S. space industry. Effective governance and rapid innovation need not be in opposition, but maintaining balance between the two requires careful policymaking.

6. Incorporate the commercial sector and other relevant nonstate actors.

It is not just governmental organizations that should play a role in managing space; the expertise and perspective of the private sector and other nonstate actors is also critical. The question of how to integrate the expertise of the private sector and nonstate actors into international organizations with a regulatory-style remit is not new. Many of the UN technical agencies set rules that commercial or private entities must follow. This is the case with ICAO and airlines, the IMO and shipping companies, and the Universal Postal Union and delivery companies.

To include private sector expertise in space traffic management, two formats look promising: an advisory group and a companion association.

Advisory group. The United States, with its partners, should lead efforts to establish a regularly scheduled forum or advisory group that channels relevant expertise from the commercial sector, civil society, and academic experts into the deliberations of responsible organizations and diplomatic efforts involving space traffic management. The United States has a long tradition of including expert private sector advisors within its own diplomatic delegations to UN functional agencies and does so at COPUOS. Policymakers could borrow from civil aviation. ICAO also has a formal Air Navigation Commission (ANC) composed of nineteen experts, which could be a model for a new permanent UNOOSA advisory function. As ICAO explains: "Although ANC Commissioners are nominated by specific ICAO Member States, and appointed by the Council, they do not represent the interest of any particular State or Region. Rather they act independently and utilize their expertise in the interest of the entire international civil aviation community." [60]

Companion association. Cooperation inside an international organization can be reinforced by a companion association. This could be designed to focus on specific issues so as to supplement, not duplicate, existing entities. Such a mechanism is particularly useful in situations in which engaging the private sector is important. This group does not need to be a formal intergovernmental entity; instead, it could be a gathering of countries, companies, experts, and other organizations.

One model for a companion association is the International Air Transport Association (IATA), the trade association for airlines, which works with airlines to implement ICAO's operational recommendations.[61] Although much of IATA's focus over the decades has been fares, in its early years, the IATA worked closely with the ICAO on air traffic safety.[62] The two organizations were intentionally located in the same city (Montreal, Canada). Today's quest to help the space industry expand safely echoes the task of setting standards for the growing airline industry decades ago.

Another model is the Major Economies Forum on Energy and Climate (MEF), which is led by governments and was convened in 2023. It provides a venue for high-level candid conversations among stakeholders before or during formal sessions of an international conference. Such an example could be expanded to include companies.

Finally, there is the Green Diplomacy Network, which the European Union spearheaded leading up to the Paris Climate Change Agreement (COP21) by using issue-focused diplomatic coordination in capitals. A more dynamic option would be to create a companion association among the most innovative countries and nonstate actors that could experiment with new ideas on space traffic management before expanding the more successful ideas to a larger group.

Whatever approach is taken, a new space companion association could take a number of actions, drawing on elements of IATA, the MEF, and the Green Diplomacy Network. It could convene national policymakers, resident diplomats, companies, and other nonstate actors in multiple capitals to confer in advance of major space decision-making conferences hosted by the ITU or UNOOSA. For example, the groups could convene every spring before the plenary session of COPUOS, held in June, and could start planning now to hold a series of meetings, beginning in 2025, to strategize in advance of the 2027 WRC.

To be effective, space management policies need to be discussed widely and deemed acceptable in different parts of the world. To that end, the new solutions developed by the companion organization could be discussed in the Group of Twenty (G20), whose members include spacefaring countries from different regions of the world. The existing G20 Space Economy Leaders Meeting, which has met in conjunction with G20 summits for five years, might provide the right context. Existing regional organizations could also provide useful venues. The African Union Commission will launch the African Space Agency in 2025, which could be another venue for such discussions.

Figure 13

Seventy-Five Nations Have Become Active in Space Since the Cold War

Countries and territories by year of first object launched into space

Launched first object by 1990 ▪ Launched first object after 1990

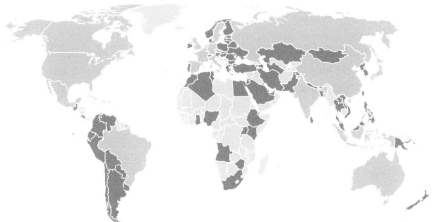

Note: Data reflects the commissioning country (i.e., the country making use of the object), which may differ from the country carrying out the launch. Data for 2024 is as of July. Data for Russia includes launches by the Soviet Union.

Source: UN Office for Outer Space Affairs.

7. Treat space as global commons.

The right to sail on the high seas beyond national jurisdiction is one of the oldest concepts in modern international relations. Accordingly, the United States should recognize space as a commons where all have a right to go—and encourage other states to do so as well.

Much like the high seas, outer space is beyond the ownership of any person, company, or government. This position is consistent with Article II of the 1967 Outer Space Treaty, which provides that outer space (including celestial bodies) "is not subject to national appropriation by claim of sovereignty, by means of use or occupation, or by any other means."

Major spacefaring countries, including China, Japan, India, Russia, the United Kingdom, and the United States, have ratified this foundational treaty. But of the ninety-six countries with objects orbiting in space (see figure 13), seventeen are not party to it.[63] For example, Djibouti is not a party to the Outer Space Treaty but is building an international commercial spaceport with a Chinese company, Hong Kong Aerospace Technology Group. Djibouti's geographical position close to the equator makes it a desirable launch location. Furthermore, a slightly different set of sixteen members of COPUOS are not party to the Outer Space Treaty.[64] Many countries, including the United States, require ratification by their legislature for a signed treaty to enter into force.

The Task Force thus recommends that all member states of the United Nations sign and ratify the Outer Space Treaty. All spacefaring states that are parties to the treaty should encourage their partners to follow suit. The norm should now be that if a state has a satellite or other item in space, or hosts a space launch site, it should be a party to the Outer Space Treaty. Eventually, that norm should expand to the point where even states that do not have items in space feel compelled to become a party.

As part of its space diplomacy, the United States could work with allies, other partners, and new spacefaring countries to improve space traffic management. In addition to its cooperation in large multilateral settings, the United States should continue to expand space diplomacy with allies and friends in other venues or configurations. The United States does not have to lead every effort. Consider the Combined Space Operations (CSpO) grouping, which marked its tenth anniversary in September 2024. CSpO brings together Australia, Canada, France, Germany, Italy, Japan, New Zealand, Norway, the United Kingdom, and the United States to improve "cooperation and coordination of national security space activities."[65]

The AUKUS allies (Australia, the United Kingdom, and the United States) have extended their cooperation into space activities. In 2023, they announced plans for the Deep Space Advanced Radar Capability, a program to enhance their ability to identify and track objects in space.[66] The United States should continue to expand inclusion of space in U.S. diplomacy.

Policymakers can bolster U.S. diplomacy by embracing the global commons concept. Differentiating between the "use" and "ownership" of the commons can help clarify application of the term. Scholar John Goehring differentiates between the concept of a commons as "enabling" versus "constraining." He notes, "referring to a global commons in a military or geopolitical context implies a focus on the *use* of an open access domain and, when used accurately, the lack of ownership is a settled question."[67] Some policymakers reject the idea of a "commons" because they fear that the concept is "constraining" and precludes extraction and ownership of resources.

However, space is beyond national jurisdiction, and all have a right of access. Civil aviation rules recognize national airspace only up to sixty thousand feet above mean sea level. Well above that level is the "Kármán line" at sixty-two miles above mean sea level, which is widely recognized as the end of the atmosphere and the beginning of space. Thus, the centuries-old concept of the high seas as a commons is enabling—everyone has a right to sail there.

Treating space as a global commons is both expedient and the right thing to do. In addition, by protecting the space interests of developing countries that are not now major spacefaring nations, U.S. advocacy of space as global commons would be popular with the nations of the Global South, adding to U.S. soft power and serving as a useful tool in the competition with China.

CONCLUSION

Policymakers in the United States and elsewhere need to recognize the strategic imperative to address the challenge of congestion and new vulnerabilities in space and make decisions now. In the coming years, more and more satellite constellations will be launched, increasing congestion in LEO. Decisions made now will affect human activity in space for years to come.

The United States must make space a top national priority and commit to revitalizing U.S. leadership in space. Advancing space management policy should be a priority for both the executive and legislative branches of government, and national leaders need to work together to fix vulnerabilities and enhance deterrence. On China, the United States will need to find effective ways to cooperate with its chief competitor to improve basic space traffic management and space safety. For now, the United States can advance an international regime of norms and standards of best practice by building on existing international organizations, forming new advisory and support mechanisms, and incorporating the private sector and other nonstate actors in space traffic management.

Dynamic companies continue to offer innovative services to more customers, but they need an orderly process for avoiding collisions in space. The space economy needs a peaceful and predictable environment, and humanity needs powerful countries to make responsible choices. The threat of miscalculation is real. The United States, China, Russia, and other spacefaring countries need clear ways to communicate their intentions. Well-managed space diplomacy can provide those communication channels. The expanding space economy and strategic calculations benefit from effective diplomacy. Despite some understandable private sector concerns about inefficient bureaucracies, creating rules of the road does not need to hamper innovation. Advances in services from space can improve life on Earth. Better rules of the road can help humanity enjoy those benefits safely.

While the new space economy needs strategic stability to thrive, people on Earth need strategic stability to survive. The United States is uniquely placed at the intersection of changing commercial, scientific, and national security needs. The United States must make space a priority now and focus on responsible leadership in humanity's newest domain.

CONCURRING OPINION

There is so much good information and knowledge in this report, and it will serve as a starting point for action by the president, working with Congress, to move this national priority forward in a timely way. For this reason, I concur with the report.

I agree with cooperating with China on safety, avoidance, and perhaps rescue in an emergency; however, there are places in the report where I disagree, and would not pursue some concepts.

First, under the recommendation to update and refine the Wolf Amendment, the modification of the amendment should not allow our scientists to confer with China and share our data without prior approval from the National Security Council or other administrative agency of the information to be shared.

Second, I agree with sharpening the policy on China to include implementing a hotline and sharing information about space traffic and working on debris mitigation. But holding joint meetings with astronauts and taikonauts or bringing joint missions to the ISS, while perhaps a possibility in the future, should not be done at this time.

Finally, regarding international regimes, I would not broaden the UN, but instead would use the Artemis Accords. The accords have the right focus, and I agree with expanding them. I would suggest giving the responsibility to the National Security Council, NASA, the Department of Defense, or other appropriate administrative agency. Additionally, with its great record of safety, I agree with using ICAO as an international regime to be modeled.

I want to thank the entire Space Task Force team for their hard work on this important national issue.

—Kay Bailey Hutchison

ENDNOTES

1. *FY25 Strategic Forces Posture: Before the Subcommittee on Strategic Forces*, 118th Cong., 2nd sess. (March 21, 2024) (statement of John F. Plumb, assistant secretary of defense for space policy), https://armedservices.house.gov/calendar/eventsingle. aspx?EventID=3554.

2. European Space Agency, "ESA Annual Space Environment Report," May 2018 and July 2024. The report shows 2,673 satellite payloads in LEO in 2018 and 11,266 in 2024.

3. Eric Berger, "SpaceX Just Stomped the Competition for a New Contract—That's Not Great," Ars Technica, July 23, 2024, https://arstechnica.com/space/2024/07/ spacex-just-stomped-the-competition-for-a-new-contract-thats-not-great/.

4. "Annual Number of Objects Launched Into Space," Our World in Data, last updated January 4, 2024, https://ourworldindata.org/grapher/yearly-number-of-objects-launched-into-outer-space. The numbers of items launched worldwide and in the United States were respectively 586 and 362 in 2019, 1,274 and 984 in 2020, and 2,664 and 2,166 in 2023.

5. Pixalytics cites the "Index of Objects Launched into Outer Space" by the UN Office for Outer Space Affairs (UNOOSA) to state 4,857 orbiting satellites in August 2018. On May 4, 2024, "Orbiting Now" listed 9,900 active satellites in Earth orbit. "How Many Satellites Are Orbiting the Earth in 2018?," Pixalytics, August 22, 2018, https://www. pixalytics.com/sats-orbiting-the-earth-2018/; "How Many Satellites are in Space?," *Kongsberg Nanoavionics* (blog), May 4, 2024, https://nanoavionics.com/blog/how-many-satellites-are-in-space/; "Orbiting Now," Orbiting Now, accessed January 23, 2025, https://orbit.ing-now.com/.

6. "Annual Number of Objects Launched Into Space," Our World in Data, https:// ourworldindata.org/grapher/yearly-number-of-objects-launched-into-outer-space, Accessed January 30, 2025. The chart lists 586 objects in 2019 and 2,664 in 2023.

7. "Types of Orbits," European Space Agency, March 3, 2020, https://www.esa.int/ Enabling_Support/Space_Transportation/Types_of_orbits#MEO.

8. Thomas G. Roberts, "Comparing Costs for Space Launch Vehicles," Aerospace Security: A Project of the Center for Strategic and International Studies, last updated September 1, 2022, accessed January 29, 2025, https://aerospace.csis.org/data/

space-launch-to-low-earth-orbit-how-much-does-it-cost/. Costs were calculated in FY21 Dollars.

9.   Brian Weeden, "2009 Iridium-Cosmos Collision Fact Sheet," Secure World Foundation, November 10, 2010, https://swfound.org/media/6575/swf_iridium_cosmos_collision_fact_sheet_updated_2012.pdf.

10. U.S. Department of State, "Russia Conducts Destructive Anti-Satellite Missile Test," news release, November 15, 2021, https://www.state.gov/russia-conducts-destructive-anti-satellite-missile-test/.

11. Scott Neuman, "A Russian Missile Creates Enough Space Junk to Pose Risk to Astronauts for Years," NPR, November 16, 2021, https://www.npr.org/2021/11/16/1056115953/russia-missile-satellite-astronaut-space-station-junk.

12. World Economic Forum, "Space Economy Set to Triple to $1.8 Trillion by 2035, New Research Reveals," news release, April 8, 2024, https://www.weforum.org/press/2024/04/space-economy-set-to-triple-to-1-8-trillion-by-2035-new-research-reveals/; World Economic Forum, In knowledge partnership with McKinsey & Company, *Space: The $1.8 Trillion Opportunity for Global Economic Growth* (Cologny, Switzerland: World Economic Forum, 2024), https://www3.weforum.org/docs/WEF_Space_2024.pdf.

13. The United States has ratified the "Treaty on Principles Governing the Activities of States in the Exploration and Use of Outer Space, including the Moon and Other Celestial Bodies," the "Agreement on the Rescue of Astronauts, the Return of Astronauts and the Return of Objects Launched Into Outer Space," the "Convention on International Liability for Damage Caused by Space Objects," and the "Convention on Registration of Objects Launched into Outer Space," but not the "Agreement Governing the Activities of States on the Moon and Other Celestial Bodies."

14. Pam Melroy, "Responsible Exploration: Preserving the Cosmos for Tomorrow," transcript of keynote address, Space Symposium, April 9, 2024, Available at https://www.youtube.com/watch?v=e75zRi3K0q4.

15. Florian Vidal, "Russia's Integrated Statecraft in the Space Domain," in *The Oxford Handbook of Space Security*, eds. Saadia Pekkanen and P. J. Blount (New York: Oxford University Press, 2024), 312–33.

16. Samuel Sanders Visner and Peter Scharfman, "Development of Cybersecurity Norms for Space Systems," American Institute of Aeronautics and Astronautics, Inc. and MITRE Corporation, 2021, paper presented at AIAA/ASCEND Conference, Las Vegas, NV, June 2023, 1–7, https://doi.org/10.48550/arXiv.2306.07441.

17. *FY25 Strategic Forces Posture: Before the Subcommittee on Strategic Forces* (statement of John F. Plumb).

18. "Treaty on Principles Governing the Activities of States in the Exploration and Use of Outer Space, Including the Moon and Other Celestial Bodies," opened for signature January 27, 1967, *UN Treaty Series Online*, registration no. 8843, https://treaties.un.org/pages/showdetails.aspx?objid=0800000280128cbd.

19. Mallory Stewart, "The Nuclear Option: Deciphering Russia's New Space Threat: Featuring Mallory Stewart, John J. Hamre, and Clayton Swope." Transcript of speech delivered at Center for Strategic and International Studies, Washington, DC, May 3,

2024, 4, https://csis-website-prod.s3.amazonaws.com/s3fs-public/2024-05/240503_Stewart_Nuclear_Option.pdf?VersionId=hon7HsECEKMjm.8UN5ke388twAnyfWij.

20. "Russia Used Its Veto to Quash a Draft Resolution Aimed at Keeping Weapons Out of Outer Space," *UN News*, April 24, 2024, https://news.un.org/en/story/2024/04/1148951.

21. United Nations, "Threat of Mass-Destruction Weapons in Space, New Technology in Military Domain Inform General Assembly's Adoption of 72 First Committee Texts," press release, December 2, 2024, https://press.un.org/en/2024/ga12660.doc.htm. See Resolution A/C.1/79/L.

22. Ibid.

23. "Chinese Space Activities Will Increasingly Challenge U.S. Interests Through 2030," Office of the Director of National Intelligence, April 2021, https://www.dni.gov/files/ODNI/documents/assessments/NICM-Declassified-Chinese-Space-Activities-through-2030--2022.pdf.

24. From 2019 through 2023, China launched 575 objects into space. "Annual Number of Objects Launched Into Space," Our World in Data.

25. Audrey Decker, "Chinese Satellites Are Breaking the U.S. 'Monopoly' on Long-Range Targeting," *Defense One*, May 2, 2024, https://www.defenseone.com/threats/2024/05/new-chinese-satellites-ending-us-monopoly-ability-track-and-hit-long-distance-targets/396272/.

26. Andrew Jones and Daisy Dobrijevic, "China's Space Station, Tiangong: A Complete Guide," *Space.com*, last updated August 15, 2023, https://www.space.com/tiangong-space-station.

27. U.S. Department of Defense, *Military and Security Developments Involving the People's Republic of China 2023, Annual Report to Congress* (Washington: U.S. Department of Defense, 2023), https://media.defense.gov/2023/Oct/19/2003323409/-1/-1/1/2023-MILITARY-AND-SECURITY-DEVELOPMENTS-INVOLVING-THE-PEOPLES-REPUBLIC-OF-CHINA.PDF.

28. *FY25 Strategic Forces Posture: Before the Subcommittee on Strategic Forces* (statement of John F. Plumb).

29. Rush Doshi, Alexis Dale-Huang, and Gaoqi Zhang, *Northern Expedition: China's Arctic Activities and Ambitions* (Washington: Brookings Institution, 2021), 1, https://www.brookings.edu/wp-content/uploads/2021/04/FP_20210412_china_arctic.pdf.

30. Ibid.

31. Andrew Jones, "Shanghai Firm Behind G60 Megaconstellation Raises $943 Million," *SpaceNews*, February 2, 2024, https://spacenews.com/shanghai-firm-behind-g60-megaconstellation-raises-943-million/.

32. Simone McCarthy, "China's Chang'e-6 Moon Mission Returns to Earth With Historic Far Side Samples," *CNN*, June 25, 2024, https://www.cnn.com/2024/06/25/china/china-change-6-moon-mission-return-scn-intl-hnk/index.html; Bruce Einhorn, "China, U.S. Are Racing to Make Billions From Mining the Moon's Minerals," Bloomberg, May 17, 2022, https://www.bloomberg.com/news/features/2022-05-17/china-us-are-in-a-space-race-to-make-billions-from-mining-the-moon-s-minerals.

33. Neil J. Cornish, "What Is a Lagrange Point," NASA, March 27, 2018, https://science.nasa.gov/resource/what-is-a-lagrange-point/.

34. Namrata Goswami and Peter A. Garretson, *Scramble for the Skies: The Great Power Competition to Control the Resources of Outer Space* (Lanham, MD: Lexington Books, October 2020), 261.

35. U.S. Department of State, "U.S. Department of State Leads Successful U.S. Delegation to World Radiocommunication Conference in Dubai," news release, December 15, 2023, https://www.state.gov/u-s-department-of-state-leads-successful-u-s-delegation-to-world-radiocommunication-conference-in-dubai/.

36. Shaun Waterman, "ITU Chief Bogdan-Martin Tasks the Satellite Industry With Expanding Internet Access," Via Satellite, March 21, 2024, https://www.satellitetoday.com/government-military/2024/03/21/itu-chief-bogdan-martin-tasks-the-satellite-industry-with-expanding-internet-access/.

37. "ICAO Space Program," ICAO, accessed December 13, 2024, https://www.icao.int/airnavigation/AeroSPACE-Transport/Pages/default.aspx.

38. Andrew Birchenough, "Marine Environmental Effects of Jettisoned Waste From Commercial Spaceflight Activities," lecture presented at the sixty-seventh session of COPUOS, Vienna, Austria, June 19–28, 2024, https://wwwcdn.imo.org/localresources/en/MediaCentre/Documents/SpaceflightLaunchDebris_Andrew%20Birchenough.pdf.

39. U.S. Department of Defense, "Joint Statement From the Combined Space Operations Initiative," news release, September 26, 2024, https://www.defense.gov/News/Releases/Release/Article/3918135/joint-statement-from-the-combined-space-operations-initiative/.

40. Saadia M. Pekkanen and P. J. Blount eds., *The Oxford Handbook of Space Security* (New York: Oxford University Press, 2024), https://doi.org/10.1093/oxfordhb/9780197582671.001.0001.

41. *Commercial Space Launch Competitiveness Act*, Public Law No: 114-90, Section 402, November 25, 2015, https://www.congress.gov/bill/114th-congress/house-bill/2262.

42. Ibid. Section 403.

43. White House, *National Security Memorandum on Critical Infrastructure Security and Resilience*, by Joseph R. Biden, Jr. (Washington: 2024), https://www.whitehouse.gov/briefing-room/presidential-actions/2024/04/30/national-security-memorandum-on-critical-infrastructure-security-and-resilience/.

44. Brian E. Humphreys, "The 2024 National Security Memorandum on Critical Infrastructure Security and Resilience," Congressional Research Service, IF12716, July 25, 2024, https://crsreports.congress.gov/product/pdf/IF/IF12716.

45. Eric Fanning, "AIA Critical Infrastructure Letter," Aerospace Industries Association, September 19, 2023, https://www.aia-aerospace.org/publications/aia-critical-infrastructure-letter/.

46. NOAA Office of Space Commerce, "Commerce Department's New Traffic Coordination System for Space Launches Initial Capabilities," news release, September

30, 2024, https://www.space.commerce.gov/
commerce-departments-new-traffic-coordination-system-for-space-launches-initial-
capabilities/.

47. Forrest E. Morgan, "Deterring Attacks on Space Systems," in *The Oxford Handbook of Space Security*, eds. Saadia M. Pekkanen and P. J. Blount (New York, NY: Oxford University Press, 2024), 204–22, https://doi.org/10.1093/oxfordhb/9780197582671.013.32.

48. The White House, "FACT SHEET: Vice President Harris Advances National Security Norms in Space," press release, April 18, 2022, https://www.presidency.ucsb.edu/documents/fact-sheet-vice-president-harris-advances-national-security-norms-space.

49. UN General Assembly, Resolution 77/41, Destructive Direct-Ascent Anti-Satellite Missile Testing, A/RES/77/41 (December 7, 2022), https://digitallibrary.un.org/record/3996915?ln=en.

50. "Destructive Direct-Ascent Anti-Satellite Missile Testing: Resolution / Adopted by the General Assembly," UN Digital Library, December 7, 2022, https://digitallibrary.un.org/record/3996915?ln=en.

51. UN General Assembly, Resolution 77/41.

52. "Station Visitors," NASA, accessed October 14, 2024, https://www.nasa.gov/international-space-station/space-station-visitors-by-country/.

53. Amber Jacobson and Elizabeth Shaw, "NASA, Artemis Accords Signatories Progress on Sustainable Exploration," NASA, accessed January 28, 2025, https://www.nasa.gov/news-release/nasa-artemis-accords-signatories-progress-on-sustainable-exploration/.

54. Richard Luscombe, "How Nasa's Artemis Accords Are Laying the Ground for Global Space Cooperation," *The Guardian*, October 20, 2024, https://www.theguardian.com/science/2024/oct/20/nasa-artemis-accords-space-diplomacy.

55. "The Artemis Accords," NASA, accessed December 13, 2024, https://www3.nasa.gov/specials/artemis-accords/.

56. United Nations Office for Outer Space Affairs, "Online Index of Objects Launched into Outer Space," accessed October 2024, https://www.unoosa.org/oosa/osoindex/search-ng.jspx?lf_id=.

57. "WRS-22: Regulation of Satellites in Earth's Orbit," *ITU News*, January 2, 2023, https://www.itu.int/hub/2023/01/satellite-regulation-leo-geo-wrs/.

58. Four of the five treaties have been widely ratified: the "Outer Space Treaty," the "Rescue Agreement," the Convention on International Liability for Damage Caused by Space Objects (the "Liability Convention"), and the Convention on Registration of Objects Launched into Outer Space (the "Registration Convention"). The fifth, the Agreement Governing the Activities of States on the Moon and Other Celestial Bodies (the "Moon Agreement"), has not been widely ratified by major space powers. "Space Law Treaties and Principles," UNOOSA, accessed January 22, 2025, https://www.unoosa.org/oosa/en/ourwork/spacelaw/treaties.html.

59. "Statement of the Delegation of Romania: Agenda Item 5: General Exchange of Views," transcript of speech delivered at sixty-seventh session of COPUOS, Vienna, Austria, June 28, 2024, https://www.unoosa.org/documents/pdf/copuos/2024/statements/5_

Romania.pdf.

60. "Air Navigation Commission," ICAO, accessed August 25, 2024, https://www.icao.int/about-icao/AirNavigationCommission/Pages/default.aspx.

61. IATA, "IATA & ICAO Extend Cooperation on Standards for Dangerous Goods Shipments," news release, January 22, 2024, https://www.iata.org/en/pressroom/2024-releases/2024-01-22-01/.

62. IATA, "Early Days," accessed October 16, 2024, https://www.iata.org/en/about/history/history-early-days/.

63. Taiwan signed the Outer Space Treaty in 1967 and ratified it in 1970. However, after the 1971 UN General Assembly vote recognizing the People's Republic of China as the representative of China, Taiwan is no longer counted as a signatory. However, Taiwan does launch satellites into space from launch pads in other countries. As of October 16, 2024, the seventeen spacefaring non-parties to the Outer Space Treaty are Angola, Bhutan, Bolivia, Costa Rica, Djibouti, Ethiopia, Ghana, Guatemala, Iran, Jordan, Latvia, Malaysia, Moldova, Monaco, Philippines, Rwanda, Taiwan, and Turkmenistan. Some countries have signed but not yet ratified the treaty, including Bolivia, Ethiopia, Ghana, Iran, Jordan, Malaysia, Philippines, and Rwanda.

64. COPUOS members who are not party to the Outer Space Treaty as of October 16, 2024, include: Albania, Angola, Bolivia, Cameroon, Chad, Costa Rica, Ethiopia, Ghana, Guatemala, Iran, Jordan, Malaysia, Philippines, Rwanda, Senegal, and Sudan. Many countries have a two-step process in which diplomats negotiate and sign a treaty then later a national legislature must approve it to legally bind the state to follow the terms of the treaty.

65. U.S. Department of Defense, "Joint Statement From the Combined Space Operations Initiative."

66. U.S. Space Force, "US, UK, Australia announce trilateral Deep Space Advanced Radar Capability initiative," news release, December 2, 2023, https://www.spaceforce.mil/News/Article-Display/Article/3604036/us-uk-australia-announce-trilateral-deep-space-advanced-radar-capability-initia/.

67. John S. Goehring, "Why Isn't Outer Space a Global Commons?," *Journal of National Security Law & Policy* 11, no. 3 (September 2021): 580, https://jnslp.com/wp-content/uploads/2021/09/Why_Isnt_Outer_Space_a_Global_Commons_2.pdf.

ACRONYMS

ANC
Air Navigation Commission

ASAT
anti-satellite weapon

AUKUS
trilateral security agreement
between Australia, the United
Kingdom, and the United States

CD
Conference on Disarmament

COP21
Paris Climate Change
Agreement

COPUOS
Committee on the Peaceful Uses
of Outer Space

CSpO
Combined Space Operations

EU
European Union

FBI
Federal Bureau of Investigation

G20
Group of Twenty

GDP
gross domestic product

GEO
geosynchronous orbit

GNSS
global navigation satellite system

GPS
Global Positioning System

IATA
International Air Transport
Association

ICAO
International Civil Aviation
Organization

ILRS
International Lunar Research
Station

IMO
International Maritime
Organization

ISS
International Space Station

ITU
International Telecommunication
Union

L$_2$
second Lagrange point

LEO
low Earth orbit

MEF
Major Economies Forum on
Energy and Climate

MEO
medium Earth orbit

NASA
National Aeronautics and Space
Administration

NOAA
National Oceanic and
Atmospheric Administration

PLA
People's Liberation Army

SBIRS
Space Based Infrared System

TraCSS
Traffic Coordination System
for Space

UN
United Nations

UNOOSA
United Nations Office for Outer
Space Affairs

WRC
World Radiocommunication
Conference

TASK FORCE MEMBERS

Task Force members are asked to join a consensus signifying that they endorse "the general policy thrust and judgments reached by the group, though not necessarily every finding and recommendation." They participate in the Task Force in their individual, not institutional, capacities.

Nina M. Armagno served thirty-five years as a national defense expert and space operations officer in the United States Air Force and the United States Space Force. As the first lieutenant general commissioned in U.S. Space Force, Armagno served as the first director of staff, where she orchestrated the establishment of the sixth branch of the U.S. Armed Forces by formulating service plans, positions, policies, and procedures. Prior to that, as the director of space programs for the assistant secretary of the air force for acquisitions, logistics, and technology, Armagno crafted comprehensive strategies to coalesce support for space programs across various governmental entities, including the Department of Defense, Congress, and the White House. She was responsible for national strategic nuclear war plans, space policies, and international engagements as the director of plans and policy at headquarters, U.S. Strategic Command. Commissioned from the U.S. Air Force Academy in 1988, she is the only person to have commanded both launch wings in the air force. Today, Armagno serves on the board of directors and strategic advisory groups for companies such as Rocket Lab, United Launch Alliance, Lockheed Martin, and VirnetX. Armagno has received a series of awards, to include the Defense Distinguished Service Medal, the General Jerome F. O'Malley Distinguished Space Leadership Award, and the Daughters of the American Revolution Patriot Award.

Charles F. Bolden Jr. served as the twelfth administrator of NASA from July 2009 until January 2017. Bolden's thirty-four-year career with the Marine Corps included fourteen years as a member of NASA's Astronaut Office and four space shuttle missions. He piloted Space Shuttle Columbia in 1986 (STS-61C) and Space Shuttle Discovery in 1990 (STS-31)—the mission that deployed the Hubble Space Telescope. He served as mission commander on Space Shuttle Atlantis in 1992 (STS-45) and Space Shuttle Discovery in 1994 (STS-60). Today, in addition to his numerous professional affiliations, Bolden serves as the founder and CEO emeritus of the Charles F. Bolden Group, providing leadership in the areas of space and aerospace exploration, national security, STEM+AD education, and health initiatives. Bolden earned a BS from the U.S. Naval Academy and an MS from the University of Southern California.

Esther D. Brimmer is the James H. Binger senior fellow in global governance at the Council of Foreign Relations. She is writing a book on the need for better governance mechanisms to manage expanding human activities in outer space. Previously, she served as project director for CFR's Task Force Report *Arctic Imperatives: Reinforcing U.S. Strategy on America's Fourth Coast.* Her career spans service in government as a senior official, as a CEO, and as a faculty member at leading universities. She led U.S. policy in international organizations as the assistant secretary of state for International Organization Affairs from 2009 to 2013 and served on the policy planning staff from 1999 to 2001. Brimmer was executive director and CEO of NAFSA: Association of International Educators from 2017 to 2022. Brimmer was the J. B. and Maurice C. Shapiro professor at George Washington University's Elliott School of International Affairs. She was the first deputy director and director of research at the Center for Transatlantic Relations at the Johns Hopkins University's Paul H. Nitze School of Advanced International Studies. Brimmer has served in the private sector as a senior advisor at McLarty Associates, and earlier as an associate at McKinsey & Company. Early in her career, she was a senior associate at the Carnegie commission on preventing deadly conflict. Brimmer received her bachelor's degree from Pomona College and master's degree and doctorate from Oxford University.

Laetitia de Cayeux is an American technology entrepreneur and investor, with a twenty-five-year career that spans the United States, Asia, and Europe. As the founder and CEO of Global Space Ventures, she funds and accelerates groundbreaking technology pioneers across domains including space, artificial intelligence, and biotechnology. An early investor in SpaceX, her impactful work as cofounder of Escape Dynamics has also been pivotal to key advancements in space and beamed energy technology. Her passion lies in leveraging technology to create large-scale, positive impacts that benefit humanity and strengthen national security. De Cayeux's leadership extends to prominent roles in influential organizations. She serves on the XPRIZE board and holds positions on the Defense Science Board of the U.S. Department of Defense, NATO Maritime Unmanned Systems Innovation Advisory Board, and the board of the National Museum of Mathematics (MoMath). Additionally, she is a member of the Economic Club of New York. She holds an MBA from ESSEC in France and Harvard Business School.

Phaedra Chrousos is the chief strategy officer of Libra Group, a privately owned international business group whose twenty subsidiaries manage and operate assets in nearly sixty countries. Libra Group is predominantly active in aerospace, renewable energy, and maritime. As chief strategy officer, Chrousos oversees a diverse portfolio of subsidiaries and leads multiple strategic initiatives. Recently, her role has expanded to include helping Libra subsidiaries integrate cutting-edge technological innovations, from piloting new use cases to placing purchase orders, into their businesses. In the past year, Chrousos successfully launched SLI, an aerospace leasing business; established LomarLabs, a maritime corporate venture lab focused on decarbonization; and contributed to the creation of Libra Philanthropies. Chrousos is a two-time venture-backed technology founder and served as a political appointee for the Barack Obama administration, where she led and scaled several of the president's digital initiatives, including 18F, and cofounded the Technology Transformation Service. Before leaving office, she coauthored the Modernizing Government Technology Act that established the federal government's $1 billion Technology Modernization Fund. Chrousos began her career as a management consultant at the Boston Consulting Group and the World Bank. She received a BA from Georgetown University, an MSc with distinction from the London School of Economics, and an MBA with honors from Columbia Business School.

Mai'a K. Davis Cross is the dean's professor of political science, international affairs, and diplomacy and director of Northeastern University's Center for International Affairs and World Cultures. A member of the Council on Foreign Relations, her work investigates processes of international cooperation, European foreign and security policy, and space diplomacy. Her work on space addresses key questions related to the geopolitics of space, the future of human space exploration, space and biotech, and public-private collaboration. She has coedited a double-length special issue on space diplomacy for the *Hague Journal of Diplomacy*, and is the author or editor of six books, including *International Cooperation Against All Odds: The Ultrasocial World, The Politics of Crisis in Europe*, and the award-winning *Security Integration in Europe: How Knowledge-Based Networks Are Transforming the European Union*. She frequently provides expert commentary through media interviews, policy briefs, and invited talks. She holds a BA in government from Harvard University and a PhD in politics from Princeton University.

Dr. Laura DeNardis is professor and endowed chair in technology, ethics, and society at Georgetown University and an acclaimed scholar of cybersecurity and internet governance. Among her many books, *The Internet in Everything: Freedom and Security in a World With No Off Switch* was listed as a *Financial Times* Top Technology Book of 2020 and her book *The Global War for Internet Governance* is considered a definitive source for understanding conflicts in cyberspace. DeNardis is an affiliated fellow of the Yale Information Society Project, where she previously served as executive director, and a senior fellow of the Centre for International Governance Innovation. She served as the research director of the Global Commission on Internet Governance from 2014 to 2016. She holds an engineering science degree from Dartmouth, an MS in engineering from Cornell, a PhD in science and technology studies from Virginia Tech, and was awarded a postdoctoral fellowship from Yale Law School.

Charles Duelfer has twenty-five years of government service involving policy, operations, and intelligence. He served at the United States Office of Management and Budget, the State Department, and CIA, focusing on regional security, nuclear weapons, and space programs. Recently he was chairman of Omnis, Inc., a consulting firm focused on intelligence analytics, training, and assorted security topics. From 2005 to 2009, he served as CEO of Transformational Space Corporation (T/Space), an entrepreneurial space launch company competing in the NASA program to develop a commercial follow-on to the Space Shuttle to supply the space station. T/Space was one of six finalists, losing to SpaceX and Orbital Sciences. Duelfer deployed to Iraq during the invasion in April 2003 and later directed the Iraq Survey Group to record the full story on the weapons of mass destruction programs (so-called Duelfer Report). He served as deputy chairman of the UN Iraq Weapons inspectorate from 1993 to 2000. Duelfer is the author of the book *Hide and Seek: The Search for Truth in Iraq*.

Celeste V. Ford is board chair and founder of Stellar Solutions, Inc., a Malcolm Baldrige National Quality Award–winning aerospace engineering company, and managing director at Stellar Ventures. Ford founded Stellar Solutions in 1995 and served as CEO until 2018 with the mission to deliver high-impact performance for defense, intelligence, commercial, civil, and international clients. She established Stellar Solutions Foundation in 1998, QuakeFinder humanitarian research and development program in 2001, and expanded Stellar's global presence with companies in the United Kingdom and France in 2003 and 2017, respectively. She launched Stellar Ventures in 2022 to invest in the next generation of space technology companies. Ford's numerous honors include lifetime achievement awards from the Baldrige Foundation and the National Association of Women Business Owners, Silicon Valley Engineering Hall of Fame, Entrepreneur of the Year from Ernst & Young, and Small Business Executive of the Year from National Defense Industry Association. Under her leadership, Stellar Solutions has been named a *Fortune* Great Place to Work since 2014. Ford is a member of numerous public, private, and nonprofit boards, including the board of trustees at the University of Notre Dame. She is an American Institute of Aeronautics and Astronautics associate fellow. She holds a BS from the University of Notre Dame and an MS from Stanford University, both in aerospace engineering.

Stephen Hadley is a principal of Rice, Hadley, Gates & Manuel LLC, an international strategic consulting firm founded with Condoleezza Rice, Robert Gates, and Anja Manuel. He is an executive vice chair of the board of directors of the Atlantic Council and is also the former board chair of the United States Institute of Peace. Hadley served as the assistant to the president for national security affairs from 2005 to 2009. From 2001 to 2005, Hadley was the assistant to the president and deputy national security advisor, serving under then National Security Advisor Condoleezza Rice. Hadley previously served on the National Security Council staff and in the Defense Department, including as assistant secretary of defense for international security policy from 1989 to 1993. During his professional career, Hadley has served on a number of corporate and advisory boards, including the National Security Advisory

Panel to the director of central intelligence, the Department of Defense Policy Board, and the State Department's Foreign Affairs Policy Board. He is also the editor of the book *Hand-Off: The Foreign Policy George W. Bush Passed to Barack Obama*.

Jane Harman served nine terms in Congress as the U.S. representative for California's 36th congressional district and was ranking member of the House Intelligence Committee after 9/11. She left the House in 2011 to become the first woman president and CEO of the Wilson Center, transitioning to president emerita in 2021. She recently chaired the Commission on the National Defense Strategy, which released a bipartisan unanimous report in July 2024. She serves on the President's Intelligence Advisory Board and is a trustee of the Aspen Institute, the Trilateral Commission, and Freedom House. Additionally, she is a distinguished fellow of the Institute of Global Politics at Columbia University's School of International and Public Affairs and a presidential scholar-in-residence at the University of Southern California's Price School of Public Policy. Harman's book, *Insanity Defense: Why Our Failure to Confront Hard National Security Problems Makes Us Less Safe*, was published in 2021.

Kay Bailey Hutchison served as the United States ambassador to NATO from 2017 to 2021. During her term, she focused on the importance of U.S. leadership in the alliance and strengthening the transatlantic bond that provides the security umbrella for Europe and North America. From 1993 to 2013, Hutchison represented Texas in the United States Senate. She was elected, by her peers, to chair the Republican Policy Committee. Kay served two terms as chair of the board of visitors at the U.S. Military Academy at West Point. She is the author of three books, including the best seller *American Heroines*. In 2013, the Dallas City Council named the city's convention center in her honor. Her alma mater, the University of Texas at Austin, named the Kay Bailey Hutchison Energy Center after her. Hutchison is the recipient of the University of Texas Presidential Citation award, the highest honor bestowed by the university. She earned a BA and JD from the University of Texas at Austin.

Rob Meyerson is the cofounder and CEO of Interlune, a company committed to sustainable and responsible harvesting of natural resources from space to benefit humanity. Meyerson is an angel investor, advisor, and/or director for companies including Axiom Space, ABL Space,

Hadrian, Hermeus, Sceye, Starfish Space, and others. Prior to Interlune, Meyerson was the president of Blue Origin and grew the company from its founding into a more than 1,500-person organization between 2003 and 2018. Prior to joining Blue Origin, Meyerson was a senior manager at Kistler Aerospace, and he began his career as an aerodynamicist at NASA's Johnson Space Center. He is an AIAA fellow, a trustee of the Museum of Flight in Seattle, and a member of the University of Michigan College of Engineering Leadership Advisory Board. For accomplishments at Blue Origin, Meyerson and his team were awarded the Robert J. Collier trophy from the National Aeronautic Association in 2016, and Meyerson was awarded the Space Flight Award by the American Astronautical Society in 2017. Meyerson earned a BS in aerospace engineering from the University of Michigan and an MS in industrial engineering from the University of Houston.

Robert B. Millard is the chairman emeritus of the MIT Corporation. He was elected to the MIT Corporation in 2003 and became the eleventh chairman of the corporation in 2014. Millard has been a member of the Visiting Committees for Physics, Architecture, Chemistry, and Philosophy and Linguistics. He also served as the chairman of MITIMCo, which manages MIT's endowment. Millard is cofounder and former chairman of the board of L3 Technologies, a major defense technology company, and currently serves as lead director of L3Harris. He is a director of Evercore, an international investment bank, and a former partner of Lehman Brothers. Millard serves on the External Advisory Council of New York University's Global Institute for Advanced Study and on the Business Advisory Board of Safar Partners. He also serves on the board of directors of the University of Engineering and Technology, Viken Technology, and Skyshow. In addition, he is a member of the MIT Dean of Science Advisory Council and the MIT Dean of Architecture and Planning Advisory Council, and is a fellow of the American Academy of Arts and Sciences. Millard attended MIT as an undergraduate and holds an MBA from Harvard Business School.

Chris Morales is a partner on the investment team at Point72 Ventures. In this role, he invests in defense tech businesses, tackling a variety of challenges related to national security. Prior to joining Point72 Ventures, Morales was a technology, media, and telecommunications associate at Goldman Sachs in its investment banking division, where he advised leading technology clients on mergers and acquisitions, debt, and equity financing. Earlier, Morales served as an F/A-18 Super Hornet weapons systems officer in the U.S. Navy, where he flew combat missions in support of Operations New Dawn and Enduring Freedom. During his last two years on active duty, he was assigned as a flight instructor responsible for teaching aircrew the techniques, tactics, and procedures of the F/A-18. Morales holds a BS in political science from the U.S. Naval Academy, a JD from the University of Pennsylvania Law School, and an MBA from the Wharton School.

Jamie Morin is vice president of defense strategic space at the Aerospace Corporation, where he leads technical support to the senior-most levels of the Department of Defense, including the U.S. Space Force and U.S. Air Force headquarters, as well as to the other military services and combatant commands. Morin also is executive director of the Center for Space Policy and Strategy, which provides objective analysis to ensure well-informed, technically defensible, and forward-looking space policy across the civil, military, intelligence, and commercial space sectors. Prior to joining Aerospace, Morin served as director of cost assessment and program evaluation (CAPE) for the Department of Defense, where he led the organization responsible for analyzing and evaluating the department's plans, programs, and budgets in relation to U.S. defense objectives, threats, estimated costs, and resource constraints. Before his appointment as director of CAPE, Morin served as assistant secretary of the air force (financial management and comptroller) and as acting undersecretary of the air force, where he led the Air Force Space Board and the Air Force Council.

Saadia M. Pekkanen is the Job and Gertrud Tamaki endowed professor of international studies, adjunct professor of political science, adjunct professor of law, and founding director of the Space Law, Data, and Policy Program at the University of Washington in Seattle. She works at the intersection of international relations and international law, specializing in the commercial, legal, and security policies shaping outer space affairs. Her regional expertise is in the foreign affairs of Japan and Asia, engaging broader themes of states, industrial policy, strategy and grand strategy, alliances, and governance in the world order. She is a member of the International Institute of Space Law. She has published eight books, as well as articles in venues such as the *American Journal of International Law Unbound*, *International Studies Quarterly*, and *International Security*. She is most recently coeditor of *The Oxford Handbook of Space Security* (2024). Pekkanen is a member of the International Institute of Space Law and a lifetime member of CFR. She earned master's degrees from Columbia University and Yale Law School and a doctorate from Harvard University in political science.

Audrey M. Schaffer is an internationally recognized expert in space policy with experience across the civil, commercial, and national security space sectors. She is currently the vice president of strategy and policy at Slingshot Aerospace, a leading space domain awareness company committed to accelerating space safety, sustainability, and security. She also is a nonresident senior associate with the Aerospace Security Project at the Center for Strategic and International Studies and a member of the Secure World Foundation advisory committee. Before joining the private sector, Schaffer served in the U.S. government for over fifteen years, holding positions in the Executive Office of the President, Department of Defense (DOD), Department of State, and NASA. She most recently was the director for space policy on the National Security Council staff. During her time in government, Schaffer led DOD efforts to establish in law the U.S. Space Force as a new branch of the armed forces, developed the U.S. policy to refrain from destructive, direct-ascent anti-satellite missile testing, and represented the United States in negotiating the first-ever UN guidelines for space sustainability. Schaffer began her career as a presidential management fellow and is a recipient of the Secretary of Defense Medal for Meritorious Civilian Service. She holds a BS in aerospace engineering from the Massachusetts Institute of Technology and an MA in international science and technology policy from the George Washington University.

Benjamin L. Schmitt is a senior fellow at the University of Pennsylvania, where he holds a joint academic appointment between the department of physics and astronomy and the Kleinman Center for Energy Policy. At Penn, Schmitt focuses on the development of the Simons Observatory, a new set of experimental cosmology telescopes and energy support infrastructure under construction at a high-altitude site in the Atacama Desert in northern Chile. At the Kleinman Center, he pursues research and teaching related to European energy security, transatlantic national security, export control policies, and modern sanctions regimes. Previously, Schmitt was a research associate and project development scientist at the Harvard-Smithsonian Center for Astrophysics, where he helped develop experimental cosmology telescopes and support infrastructure at the South Pole. For this work, he traveled to the Amundsen-Scott South Pole Station in Antarctica and is a recipient of the U.S. Antarctica Service Medal. Schmitt remains an affiliate of the Harvard-Smithsonian Center for Astrophysics and is also an associate of the Harvard-Ukrainian Research Institute. He is cofounder of the Duke University Space Diplomacy Lab and is also a senior fellow at the Center for European Policy Analysis. He previously served as European energy security advisor at the U.S. Department of State and received his PhD in physics and astronomy from the University of Pennsylvania.

Jonathan Spalter is president and CEO of USTelecom–The Broadband Association, the national trade association representing technology providers, innovators, suppliers, and manufacturers committed to connecting the world through the power of broadband. Prior to joining USTelecom, he served as chair of Mobile Future, the national wireless technology association. He has held key leadership positions in the executive branch of government. Spalter was confirmed by the U.S. Senate as associate director of the U.S. Information Agency and managed the agency's global technology resources as chief information officer. He also was a policy aide to the undersecretary of defense for policy at the Pentagon. In the private sector, Spalter's executive roles included CEO of Snocap, the digital content services company founded by the creators of Napster. He also was CEO of Atmedica Worldwide, the online health-care affiliate of the *Fortune 100* telecommunications and media company Vivendi Universal, where he also served as executive vice president for business development and strategy at its internet subsidiary VivendiNet, and as the group's senior vice president for global public policy. Spalter is a graduate of Harvard College and Cambridge University and has served as an advisor to and board member of cutting-edge technology companies, financial institutions, and nonprofit organizations in Silicon Valley and beyond.

Kathryn D. Sullivan has a long career as a distinguished scientist, astronaut, and executive. She was one of the first six women to join NASA's astronaut corps in 1978 and holds the distinction of being the first American woman to walk in space. Her submersible dive to the Challenger Deep in June of 2020 made her a triple Guinness World Record holder—as the most vertical person in the world, the first person to both orbit the planet and reach its deepest point, and the first woman to dive to full ocean depth. Sullivan has held a variety of senior executive and advisory positions since leaving NASA, the most recent of which is her September 2021 appointment to the President's Council of Advisors on Science and Technology. Previous positions include presidential appointments as undersecretary of commerce for oceans and atmosphere and administrator of the National Oceanic and Atmospheric Administration (NOAA) in 2014, NOAA deputy administrator in 2011, NOAA chief scientist in 1993, and member of the National Science Board in 2004. She currently serves on the boards of International Paper, Accenture Federal Services, Terra Alpha Investments, and the National Audubon Society. She is also a senior fellow at the Potomac Institute for Policy Studies and ambassador-at-large for the Smithsonian Institution's National Air and Space Museum. She has been awarded the Nevada Medal, the Explorers Club Medal, the Rachel Carson Award, an Emmy, and nine honorary degrees, and is the author of the children's books *To the Stars!*, *Handprints on Hubble: An Astronaut's Story of Invention*, and *How to Spacewalk*. Sullivan earned a BS in Earth sciences from University of California at Santa Cruz and a PhD in geology from Dalhousie University, Nova Scotia.

Ezinne Uzo-Okoro is a senior fellow at Harvard University's Belfer Center for Science and International Affairs and a Venture Partner at SineWave Ventures. She serves on the board of the QinetiQ Group PLC, a global defense company. She spent twenty years in government contributing to both NASA missions and policy. Uzo-Okoro drove innovation in space and aeronautics at the White House Office of Science and Technology Policy. Her policy work includes Earth observations, orbital debris, microgravity research in low Earth orbit, space weather, in-space servicing assembly and manufacturing, aeronautics, and space science. Her seventeen-year NASA engineering career spanned contributions to Earth observations, planetary science, heliophysics, astrophysics, human exploration, and space communications missions. She is a CFR term member, and is a recipient of several NASA awards and the Commercial Space Federation Commercial Space Policy award. She earned an undergraduate degree in computer science from Rensselaer Polytechnic Institute, and master's degrees in aerospace systems, space robotics, and public policy from Johns Hopkins University, MIT's Media Lab, and Harvard University, respectively. She also earned a doctorate degree in aeronautics and astronautics from MIT.

Samuel S. Visner serves as chair of the board of directors of the Space Information Sharing and Analysis Center and as a technical fellow at the Aerospace Corporation. Visner is also a senior advisor to the Cybersecurity Solarium Commission. He served previously as director of the National Cybersecurity Federally Funded Research and Development Center, operated by MITRE and sponsored by the National Institute of

Standards and Technology. Visner held prior roles as senior vice president at ICF and head of cybersecurity and resilience, vice president at CSC and general manager of CSC Global Cybersecurity, senior vice president at SAIC, and as chief of Signals Intelligence Programs at the National Security Agency, from which he received the agency's highest award for civilian service in recognition of work done to transform the agency's signals intelligence infrastructure following 9/11. He served as an adjunct professor at Georgetown University, where he taught a course on cybersecurity policy, operations, and technology, and has also established a charitable trust for the university for the continued development of curricula in the study of information technology in international security. He is a member of the board of directors of the Oak Ridge Associated Universities and also serves as a member of the Cyber Council of the Intelligence and National Security Alliance and the Cyber Committee of the Armed Forces Communications and Electronics Association. He is a member of the Atlantic Council, a member of the Army Science Board, and a former member of the Intelligence Community Studies Board. Visner holds a BA in international politics from Georgetown University and an MA in telecommunications from George Washington University.

TASK FORCE OBSERVERS

Observers participate in Task Force discussions but are not asked to join the consensus. They participate in their individual, not institutional, capacities.

Laura Delgado López is a policy advisor at NASA's Science Mission Directorate's policy branch, which provides policy support to the science leadership of the agency. She previously worked as a senior policy analyst in the policy branch. In September 2024, she completed her visiting fellowship with the Americas program at the Center for Strategic and International Studies (CSIS), where she researched international space cooperation in Latin America. Her tenure at CSIS was funded by a CFR international affairs fellowship. She has worked in space policy for fifteen years. Her research on space politics and policy has focused on emerging space programs, international cooperation, and public opinion, and has been featured in peer-reviewed and trade publications. Prior to NASA, she was an advocacy lead at Harris Corporation's Space and Intelligence Systems Segment, a project manager at the Secure World Foundation, the Earth observations associate at the Institute for Global Environmental Strategies, and a correspondent for *SpacePolicyOnline.com*. Delgado López is a former editor-in-chief of Elsevier's *Space Policy Journal*. She holds a BA in political science from the University of Puerto Rico and an MA in international science and technology policy with a focus on space policy from George Washington University.

Kat Duffy is a senior fellow for digital and cyberspace policy at the Council on Foreign Relations. Duffy has more than two decades of experience operating at the nexus of emerging technology, democratic principles, corporate responsibility, and human rights. She has implemented, overseen, and/or funded foreign assistance and philanthropic initiatives across more than sixty countries, with a particular focus on supporting anti-censorship technologies, digital rights advocacy, independent media, and the digital safety of human rights defenders, journalists, and civil society organizations. She served for five years on the board of the Global Network Initiative, a multistakeholder initiative driving voluntary principles for technology companies to support free expression and privacy rights, and regularly advises governments, nongovernmental organizations, and the private sector on crafting strategic responses to emerging technology policy. Duffy received her BA from Yale University and her JD from the University of Michigan.

Liana Fix is a fellow for Europe at the Council on Foreign Relations. She is a historian and political scientist with expertise in German and European foreign and security policy, European security, transatlantic relations, Russia, Eastern Europe, and European China policy. Fix is the author of *A New German Power? Germany's Role in European Russia Policy.* She is an adjunct faculty member at Georgetown University's Center for German and European Studies and Center for Eurasian, Russian, and East European Studies. Prior to CFR, Fix was Körber-Stiftung's program director for international affairs in Berlin. She was also a resident fellow at the German Marshall Fund, a DAAD/AICGS fellow at the American Institute for Contemporary German Studies, a fellow for global governance futures at the Robert Bosch Foundation Multilateral Dialogues, a doctoral fellow at the German Institute for International and Security Affairs, and an associate fellow at the German Council on Foreign Relations. Fix has contributed essays and articles to journals including *Foreign Affairs* and *Foreign Policy.* Fix received her MSc in theory and history of international relations from the London School of Economics and Political Science and her PhD in political science from the Justus Liebig University Giessen.

Rachel Lindbergh is a space policy analyst at the Congressional Research Service, a legislative branch agency that provides Congress with objective, nonpartisan analysis. Prior to 2023, Lindbergh conducted space policy research for the Institute for Defense Analyses Science and Technology Policy Institute (STPI), a federally funded research and development center that provides objective research to the White House Office of Science and Technology Policy and federal agencies with a science and technology mission. At STPI, Lindbergh's research spanned civil, commercial, and defense space policy, including norms of behavior in space, economic trends in Earth orbit and cislunar space, Russian space capabilities, planetary protection, and global competition in space. Prior to STPI, Lindbergh worked for the International Space Station National Laboratory, conducting an assessment of macromolecular crystallography research conducted in microgravity. She also conducted metallurgical research on the International Space Station as a principal investigator. Her experience was profiled in the *Atlantic*, and in 2022, she gave a TEDx on space policy. Lindbergh received her BA in public policy and Russian and Eastern European studies at the University of Chicago, writing an honors thesis on the commercialization of low Earth orbit.

Zongyuan Zoe Liu is the Maurice R. Greenberg senior fellow for China studies at the Council on Foreign Relations. Her work focuses on international finance, sovereign wealth funds, industrial policies, and the geoeconomics of energy transition. Liu is the author of *Can BRICS De-dollarize the Global Financial System?* and *Sovereign Funds: How the Communist Party of China Finances Its Global Ambitions. Sovereign Funds* was the 2024 winner of the PROSE Award in business, finance, and management. Liu is an adjunct assistant professor at Columbia University's School of International and Public Affairs. Prior to joining CFR, Liu was an assistant professor at Texas A&M's Bush School of Government and Public Service in Washington, DC. She joined the Bush School after post doctoral fellowships at the Columbia-Harvard China and the World Program and the Center for International Environment and Resource Policy at Tufts University's Fletcher School. She is also a chartered financial analyst charterholder. Her paper *BRICS Collective De-dollarization Statecraft* received the 2021 Best Paper Award from the International Studies Association (West) annual conference. Liu received her PhD in international relations from Johns Hopkins University.

Manjari Chatterjee Miller is a senior fellow for India, Pakistan, and South Asia at the Council on Foreign Relations; professor of international relations at the University of Toronto's Munk School of Global Affairs and Public Policy, where she holds the inaugural Munk Chair in Global India; and associate at Harvard University's Asia Center. She is the author of *Why Nations Rise: Narratives and the Path to Great Power, Wronged by Empire: Post-Imperial Ideology and Foreign Policy in India and China*, and coeditor of the *Routledge Handbook of China-India Relations*. Miller also previously held faculty and/or research positions at Boston

University, the Atlantic Council, the Belfer Center for Science and International Affairs, the National University of Singapore, the Chinese Academy of Social Sciences, and the Australian National University. She serves on the international advisory board of Chatham House's *International Affairs* journal and the editorial board of the National Bureau of Asian Research's *Asia Policy* journal and was a *Hindustan Times* columnist until 2024. Miller received her BA from the University of Delhi, MSc from the University of London, and PhD from Harvard University. She was a post doctoral fellow in Princeton University's China and the World Program.

Ryan Pettit serves as professional staff member on the U.S. Senate Defense Appropriations Subcommittee. A Senate staffer since 2008, he previously served on the Budget Committee, Veterans' Affairs Committee, and as Senator Patty Murray's (D-WA) senior national security advisor. As a civil affairs specialist in the Marine Corps, he deployed to Ramadi and Habbaniyah, Iraq, and Helmand, Afghanistan. Pettit has been awarded the Combat Action Ribbon and the Navy and Marine Corps Achievement Medal, three awards with combat 'V,' three times. He received a BA from George Mason University, an MA in strategic security studies from the National Defense University, and an MA degree in strategic studies from the Johns Hopkins School of Advanced International Studies.

Matthew Pylypciw is a professional staff member on the House Permanent Select Committee on Intelligence. Prior to joining the committee in 2021, Matthew served as an acquisition program manager at the National Reconnaissance Office (NRO) as an air force officer and later as a government civilian. Before his assignment at the NRO, he managed the Global Positioning System as a satellite operator at Schriever Air Force Base in Colorado. He continues to serve in the air force reserves. Matthew holds a bachelor of science degree from Penn State and a master of public management degree from the University of Maryland.

Anya Schmemann is managing director of global communications and of the Task Force Program at the Council on Foreign Relations in Washington, DC. At CFR, Schmemann has overseen numerous high-level Task Forces on a wide range of topics, including cybersecurity, China's Belt and Road, pandemic preparedness, innovation, the future of work, Arctic strategy, nuclear weapons, climate change, immigration, trade policy, and internet governance, as well as on U.S. policy toward Afghanistan, Brazil, North Korea, Pakistan, and Turkey. She previously served as assistant dean for communications and outreach at American University's School of International Service and managed communications at Harvard Kennedy School's Belfer Center for Science and International Affairs, where she also administered the Caspian studies program. She coordinated a research project on Russian security issues at the EastWest Institute in New York and was assistant director of CFR's Center for Preventive Action in New York, focusing on the Balkans and Central Asia. She was a Truman National Security fellow and is chair of the Global Kids DC advisory council. Schmemann received a BA in government and an MA in Russian studies from Harvard University.

Sheila A. Smith is John E. Merow senior fellow for Asia-Pacific studies at the Council on Foreign Relations. She is the author of *Japan Rearmed: The Politics of Military Power, Intimate Rivals: Japanese Domestic Politics and a Rising China,* and *Japan's New Politics and the U.S.-Japan Alliance.* Smith is the author of the CFR interactive guide *Constitutional Change in Japan* and contributor to CFR's *Asia Unbound* blog. Smith joined CFR from the East-West Center, where she directed multinational research in a study of the domestic politics of the U.S. military presence in Japan, the Philippines, and South Korea. She was a visiting scholar at Keio University researching Japan's foreign policy toward China. Smith has been a visiting researcher at the Japan Institute of International Affairs, the Research Institute for Peace and Security, the University of Tokyo, and the University of the Ryukyus. Smith was the chair of the Japan-U.S. Friendship Commission and the U.S. advisors to the U.S.-Japan Conference on Cultural and Educational Interchange. She is an adjunct professor at Georgetown University's Asian studies department and serves on the board of its *Journal of Asian Affairs.* Smith earned her MA and PhD from Columbia University's political science department.

Mike Wakefield serves as a professional staff member and senior counsel to the U.S. Senate Committee on Appropriations. He previously served as senior counsel to Senator Susan Collins (R-ME) and as legislative counsel to former Representative Mike Coffman, where he handled the defense, homeland security, and veterans' affairs portfolios. Before joining Representative Coffman's staff in 2015, he served in the U.S. Army as assistant counsel for legislation, fiscal, and general law and earlier as a military social aide to the president. Wakefield received a BS in commerce from the University of Virginia and a JD from the University of Virginia School of Law.

Contributing CFR Staff

Dalia Albarrán
Associate Director,
Graphic Design

María Teresa Alzuru
Deputy Director,
Product Management

Sabine Baumgartner
Senior Photo Editor

Michael Bricknell
Data Systems Designer

Patricia Lee Dorff
Managing Director, Publications

Julia Katsovich
Research Associate,
International Institutions
and Global Governance

Will Merrow
Associate Director,
Data Visualization

Caitlin Moran
Senior Editor, Publications

Anya Schmemann
Managing Director,
Task Force Program

Justin Schuster
Associate Producer,
Video and Audio

Chelie Setzer
Deputy Director,
Task Force Program

Katerina Viyella
Program Associate,
Task Force Program

Contributing Interns

Davide Donald
International Institutions
and Global Governance

Jude A. Farley
Task Force Program

Meghan Ford-Titus
Task Force Program

Emma C. Gargiulo
Task Force Program

Alexandra Huggins
International Institutions
and Global Governance

Catherine Plywaczewski
International Institutions
and Global Governance